Dayaream

www.randomhousechildrens.co.uk

Jacqueline Wilson

Jacky Daydream

Illustrated by Nick Sharratt

CORGI YEARLING

JACKY DAYDREAM
A CORGI YEARLING BOOK 978 0 440 86720 3

First published in Great Britain by Doubleday,
an imprint of Random House Children's Publishers UK
A Random House Group Company

Doubleday edition published 2007
Corgi Yearling edition published 2008

7 9 10 8

Corgi Yearling Books are published by Random House Children's Publishers UK,
61–63 Uxbridge Road, London W5 5SA

www.**randomhousechildrens**.co.uk

Addresses for companies within The Random House Group Limited can be found at:
www.randomhouse.co.uk/offices.htm

THE RANDOM HOUSE GROUP Limited Reg. No. 954009

A CIP catalogue record for this book is available from the British Library.

The Random House Group Limited supports The Forest Stewardship Council (FSC®), the
leading international forest certification organisation. Our books carrying the FSC label are
printed on FSC® certified paper. FSC is the only forest certification scheme endorsed by the
leading environmental organisations, including Greenpeace. Our paper procurement policy can
be found at www.randomhouse.co.uk/environment

Printed and bound by CPI Group (UK) Ltd, Croydon, CR0 4YY

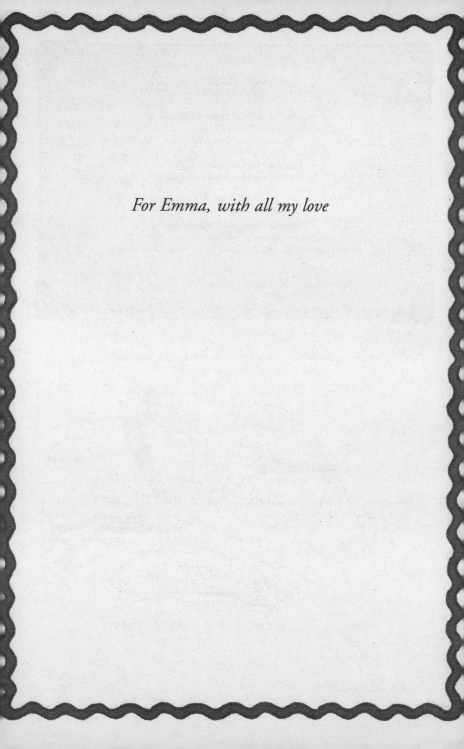

For Emma, with all my love

17th December 1945

1

Birth!

I was more than a fortnight late for my own birth. I was due at the beginning of December and I didn't arrive until the seventeenth. I don't know why. It isn't at all like me. I'm always very speedy and I can't stand being late for anything.

My mum did her level best to get me going. She drank castor oil and skipped vigorously every morning. She's a small woman – five foot at most in her high heels. She was nearly as wide as she was long by this time. She must have looked like a beach ball. It's a wonder they didn't try to bounce the baby out.

When I eventually got started, I still took forty-eight hours to arrive. In fact they had to pull me out with forceps. They look like a medieval instrument of torture. It can't have been much fun for my mother – or me. The edge of the forceps caught my mouth. When I was finally yanked out into the harsh white light of the delivery room in the hospital, my mouth was lopsided and partially paralysed.

They didn't bother about mothers and babies bonding in those days. They didn't give us time to

1

have a cuddle or even take a good look at each other. I was bundled up tightly in a blanket and taken off to the nursery.

I stayed there for four days without a glimpse of my mother. The nurses came and changed my nappy and gave me a bath and tried to feed me with a bottle, though it hurt my sore mouth.

I wonder what I thought during those long lonely first days. I'm sure babies *do* think, even though they can't actually say the words. What would I do now if I was lying all by myself, hungry and frightened? That's easy. I'd make up a story to distract myself. So maybe I started pretending right from the day I was born.

I imagined my mother bending over my cot, lifting me up and cradling her cheek against my wispy curls. Each time a nurse held me against her starched white apron I'd shut my eyes tight and pretend *she* was my mother, soft and warm and protective. I'd hope she'd keep me in her arms for ever. But she'd pop me back in my cot and after three or four hours another nurse would come and I'd have to start the whole game all over again.

So perhaps I tried a different tack. Maybe I decided I didn't need a mother. If I could only find the right spell, drink the necessary magic potion, my bendy baby legs would support me. I could haul myself out of the little metal cot, pack a bag with a spare nappy and a bottle, wrap myself up warm in my new hand-knitted matinée jacket and patter over the polished floor. I'd go out of the nursery, down the corridor, bump myself down the stairs on my padded bottom and out of the main entrance into the big wide world.

What was my mother thinking all this time? She was lying back in her bed, weepy and exhausted, wondering why they wouldn't bring her baby.

'She can't feed yet, dear. She's got a poorly mouth,' said the nurses.

My mum imagined an enormous scary wound, a great gap in my face.

'I thought I'd given birth to a monster,' my mum told me later. 'I wasn't sure I *wanted* to see you.'

But then, on the fourth day after my birth, one of the doctors discovered her weeping. He told her the monster fears were nonsense.

'I'll go and get your baby myself,' he said.

He went to the nursery, scooped me out of my cot and took me to my mother. She peered at me anxiously. My mouth was back in place, just a little sore at the edge. My eyes were still baby blue and wide open because I wanted to take a good look at my mother now I had the chance. I wasn't tomato red and damp like a newborn baby. I was now pink-and-white and powdered and my hair was fluffy.

'She's pretty!' said my mum. 'She's just like a little doll.'

My mum had always loved dolls as a little girl. She'd played with them right up until secondary school. She loved dressing them and undressing them and getting them to sit up straight. But I was soft flesh, not hard china. My mother cradled me close.

My dad came and visited us in hospital. Fathers didn't get involved much with babies in those days but he held me gently in his big broad hands and gave me a kiss.

My grandma caught the train from Kingston up to London, and then she got on a tube, and then she took the Paddington train to Bath, where we lived, and then a bus to the hospital, just to catch a glimpse of her new granddaughter. It must have taken her practically all day to get there because transport was slow and erratic just after the war.

She was a trained milliner, very nifty with a needle, quick at knitting, clever at crochet. She came with an enormous bag of handmade baby clothes, all white, with little embroidered rosebuds, a very special Christmas present when there was strict clothes rationing and you couldn't find baby clothes for love nor money.

I had my first Christmas in hospital, with pastel-coloured paperchains drooping round the ward and a little troop of nurses with lanterns singing carols and a slice of chicken and a mince pie for all the patients. This was considered a feast as food was still rationed too. Luckily my milk was free and I could feed at last.

Can you think of a Jacqueline Wilson book where the main character has a little chat even though she's a newborn baby?

It's Gemma, in my book *Best Friends*. Gemma chats a great deal, especially to Alice. They've been best friends ever since the day they were born. Gemma is born first, at six o'clock in the morning, and then Alice is born that afternoon. They're tucked up next to each other that night in little cots.

I expect Alice was a bit frightened. She'd have cried. She's actually still a bit of a crybaby now but I try not to tease her about it. I always do my best to comfort her.

I bet that first day I called to her in baby-coo language. I'd say, 'Hi, I'm Gemma. Being born is a bit weird, isn't it? Are you OK?'

I often write about sad and worrying things in my books, like divorce and death – though I try hard to be as reassuring as possible, and I always like to have funny parts. I want you to laugh as well as cry. One of the saddest things that can happen to you when you're a child is losing your best friend, and yet even the kindest of adults don't always take this seriously.

'Never mind, you'll quickly make a *new* best friend,' they say.

They don't have a clue how lonely it can be at school without a best friend and how you can ache with sadness for many months. In *Best Friends* I tried hard to show what it's really like – but because Gemma is pretty outrageous it's also one of my funniest books too. I like Gemma and Alice a lot, but I'm particularly fond of Biscuits.

He's my all-time favourite boy character. He's so kind and gentle and full of fun, and he manages not to take life too seriously. Of course he eats too much, but I don't think this is such an enormous sin. Biscuits will get tuned in to healthy eating when he's a teenager, but meanwhile I'm glad he enjoys his food. His cakes look delicious!

2

My Mum and Dad

I was fine. My mum was fine. We could go home now.

We didn't really have a *proper* home, a whole house we owned ourselves. My mum and dad had been sent to Bath during the war to work in the Admiralty. He was a draughtsman working on submarine design, she was a clerical officer. They met at a dance in the Pump Room, which sounds like part of a ship but is just a select set of rooms in the middle of the city where they had a weekly dance in wartime.

My mum and dad danced. My mum, Biddy, was twenty-one. My dad, Harry, was twenty-three. They went to the cinema and saw *Now, Voyager* on their first proper date. Biddy thought the hero very dashing and romantic when he lit two cigarettes in his mouth and then handed one to his girl. Harry didn't smoke and he wasn't one for romantic gestures either.

However, they started going out together. They went to the Admiralty club. They must have spun out a lemonade or two all evening because neither of them drank alcohol. I only ever saw them down a small glass of Harvey's Bristol Cream sherry at Christmas. They went for walks along the canal together. Then Harry proposed and Biddy said yes.

I don't think it was ever a really grand passionate true love.

'It wasn't as if you had much choice,' Biddy told me much later. 'There weren't many men around, they were all away fighting. I'd got to twenty-one, and in those days you were starting to feel as if you were on the shelf if you weren't married by then. So I decided your father would do.'

'But what did you like about Harry?'

My mum had to think hard. 'He had a good sense of humour,' she said eventually.

I suppose they did have a laugh together. Once or twice.

Harry bought Biddy an emerald and diamond ring. They were very small stones, one emerald and two diamonds, but lovely all the same.

They didn't hang about once they were engaged. They got married in December. Biddy wore a long white lace dress and a veil, a miracle during wartime, when many brides had to make do with short dresses made out of parachute silk. She had a school friend who now lived in Belfast, where you didn't need coupons for clothes. She got the length of lace and my grandma made it up for her.

She had little white satin shoes – size three – and a bouquet of white roses. Could they have been real roses in December during the war? No wonder my mother is holding her bouquet so proudly. Harry looks touchingly proud too, with this small pretty dark-haired girl holding his arm. They'd only known each other three months and yet here they were, standing on the steps of St John's Church in Kingston, promising to love and honour each other for a lifetime.

They had a few days' honeymoon in Oxford and then they went back to Bath. They'd lived in separate digs before, so now they had to find a new home to start their married life together. They didn't have any money and there weren't any houses up for sale anyway. It was wartime.

They went to live with a friend called Vera, who had two children, but when my Mum quickly became pregnant with me, Vera said they'd have to go.

'No offence, but there's not room for two prams in my hall. You'll have to find some other digs.'

They tramped the streets of Bath but my mother had started to show by this time. All the landladies looked at her swollen stomach and shook their heads.

'No kiddies,' each said, over and over.

They must have been getting desperate, and now

they only had one wage between them, because Biddy had to resign from work when people realized she was pregnant. There was no such thing as maternity leave in those days.

Eventually they found two rooms above a hairdresser's. The landlady folded her arms and sucked her teeth when she saw Biddy's stomach, but said they could stay as long as she didn't ever hear the baby crying. She didn't want her other lodgers disturbed.

Biddy promised I'd be a very quiet baby. I was, reasonably so. Harry came to collect Biddy and me from the hospital. We went back to our two furnished rooms on the bus. We didn't have a car. We'd have to wait sixteen years for one. But Harry did branch out and buy a motorized tandom bike and sidecar, a weird lopsided contraption. Biddy sensibly considered this too risky for a newborn baby.

I was her top priority now.

Which of my books starts with a heavily pregnant mum trying to find a new home for her daughters?

12

It's *The Diamond Girls*. That mum has four daughters already: Martine, Jude, Rochelle and Dixie. She's about to give birth to the fifth little Diamond and she's certain this new baby will be a boy.

'I've got a surprise for you girls,' said Mum. 'We're moving.'

We all stared at her. She was flopping back in her chair, slippered feet propped right up on the kitchen table amongst the cornflake bowls, tummy jutting over her skirt like a giant balloon. She didn't look capable of moving herself as far as the front door. Her scuffed fluffy mules could barely support her weight. Maybe she needed hot air underneath her and then she'd rise gently upwards and float out of the open window.

I'm very fond of that mum, Sue Diamond, but *my* mum would probably call her Common as Muck. Sue believes in destiny and tarot cards and fortune-telling. My mum would think it a Load of Old Rubbish.

I wonder which Diamond daughter you feel I'm most like? I think it's definitely dreamy little Dixie.

3

Babyhood

Biddy settled down happily to being a mother. I was an easy baby. I woke up at night, but at the first wail my mum sat up sleepily, reached for me and started feeding me. She had a lamp on and read to keep herself awake: *Gone with the Wind*; *Forever Amber*; *Rebecca*. Maybe I craned my neck round mid-guzzle and tried to read them too. I read all three properly when I was thirteen or so but I wasn't really a girl for grand passion. Poor Biddy, reading about dashing heroes like Rhett Butler and Max de Winter with Harry snoring on his back beside her in his winceyette pyjamas.

I didn't cry much during the day. I lay in my pram, peering up at the ceiling. At the first sign of weak sunshine in late February I was parked in the strip of garden outside. All the baby books reckoned fresh air was just as vital as mother's milk. Babies were left outside in their big Silver Cross prams, sometimes for hours on end. If they cried, they were simply 'exercising their lungs'. You'd never leave a pram outside in a front garden now. You'd be terrified of strangers creeping in and wheeling the baby away. But it was the custom then, and you 'aired' your babies just like you did your washing.

There was a *lot* of washing. There were no disposable nappies in those days so all my cloth nappies had to be washed by hand. There were no washing machines either, not for ordinary families like us, anyway. There wasn't even constant hot water from the tap.

Biddy had to boil the nappies in a large copper pan, stirring them like a horrible soup, and then fishing them out with wooden tongs. Then she'd wash them again and rinse them three times, with a dab of 'bluebag' in the last rinse to make them look whiter than white. Then she'd hang them on the washing line to get them blown dry and properly aired. Then she'd pin one on me and I'd wet it and she'd have to start all over again. She had all her own clothes to wash by hand, and Harry's too – all his white office shirts, and his tennis and cricket gear come the summer – and I had a clean outfit from head to toe every single day, sometimes two or three.

I wore such a lot of clothes too. In winter there was the nappy and rubber pants, and then weird knitted knickers called a pilch, plus a vest and a liberty bodice to protect my chest, and also a binder when I was a very young baby (I think it was meant to keep my belly button in place). Then there was a petticoat, and then a long dress down past my feet, and then a hand-knitted fancy matinée jacket. Outside in winter there'd be woolly booties and matching mittens and a bonnet and several blankets and a big crocheted shawl. Perhaps it was no wonder I was a docile baby and didn't cry much. I could scarcely expand my lungs to draw breath wearing that little lot.

They were all snowy white and every single garment was immaculately ironed even though all I did was lie on them and crease them. My mother took great pride in keeping me clean. She loved it when people admired my pristine appearance when she wheeled me out shopping. She vaguely knew Patricia Dimbleby, Richard Dimbleby's sister, David and Jonathan Dimbleby's aunt (all three men are famous broadcasters), and plucked up the courage to ask her for tea.

I wonder what she gave her. Milk was rationed. Biscuits were rationed. Did she manage to make rock cakes using up her whole week's butter and sugar and egg allowance? Still, the visit was a success, whatever the sacrifice. Sixty years later my mum's face still glows when she talks about that visit.

'She positively *gushed* over you. She said she'd never seen such a clean baby, so perfectly kept, everything just so. She said I was obviously a dab hand at washing and ironing.'

It's interesting that the one children's classic picture book my mother bought for me was Beatrix Potter's *Mrs Tiggywinkle*. My mother didn't like animals: 'Too dirty, too noisy, too smelly.' She usually turned her nose up at children's books about animals, but though Mrs Tiggywinkle was undoubtedly a hedgehog, she was also a washerwoman, and a very good one too.

Which baby in one of my books is discovered without any clothes at all on the day she is born?

It's April, in *Dustbin Baby*. She's abandoned by her mother, thrust into a dustbin the moment she's born.

I cry and cry and cry until I'm as red as a raspberry, the veins standing out on my forehead, my wisps of hair damp with effort. I am damp all over because I have no nappy. I have no clothes at all and if I stop crying I will become dangerously cold.

I've always wondered what it must be like not to know your own family. Imagine being told to crayon your family tree at school and not having a single name to prop on a branch. April doesn't know who her mother is, who her father is. She doesn't know who *she* is. So she sets out on her fourteenth birthday to find out.

4

Housewife's Choice

Biddy didn't just keep me sparkling clean. She fussed around our rented flat every day after breakfast, dusting and polishing and carpet-sweeping. She didn't wear a turban and pinny like most women doing dusty work. She thought they looked common.

She listened to the Light Programme on the big wooden radio, tuning in to *Housewife's Choice*, singing along to its signature tune, *doobi-do do doobi-do*, though she couldn't sing any song in tune, not even 'Happy Birthday'.

When she was done dusting, we went off to the shops together. You couldn't do a weekly shop in those days. We didn't have a fridge and there was so little food in the shops, you couldn't stock up. You had to queue everywhere, and smile and simper at the butcher, hoping he might sell you an extra kidney or a rabbit for a stew. Biddy was pert and pretty so she often got a few treats. One day, when he had no lamb chops, no neck or shoulder, he offered my mum a sheep's head.

She went home with it wrapped in newspaper,

precariously balanced on the pale green covers of my pram. She cleaned the head as best she could, holding it at arm's length, then shoved it in the biggest saucepan she could find. She boiled it and boiled it and boiled it, then fished it out, hacked at it and served it up to Harry with a flourish when he came back from work.

He looked at the chunks of strange stuff on his plate and asked what it was. She was silly enough to tell him. He wouldn't eat a mouthful. I was very glad I still had milk for my meals.

She couldn't go back to the butcher's for a few days as she'd had more than her fair share of meat, so she tried cutting the head up small and swooshing it around with potatoes and carrots, turning it into sheep soup.

Harry wasn't fooled. There was a big row. He shouted that he wasn't ever going to eat that sort of muck. She screamed that she was doing her best – what did he expect her to do, conjure up a joint of beef out of thin air? He sulked. She wept. I curled up in my cot and sucked my thumb.

There were a lot of days like that. But in the first photos in the big black album we are smiling smiling smiling, playing Happy Families. There are snapshots of days out on the tandem, blurred pictures of me squinting in the sunlight but still smiling. I'm in my summer woollies now, still wearing several layers, but at least my legs are bare so I can kick on my rug.

There are professional photos of me lying on my tummy, stripped down to my knitted knickers, smiling obediently while Biddy and the photographer clapped and cavorted. There are pictures of me sitting up on the grass but I always have a little rug under me to keep me clean. There's even a photo of me in my tiny tin bath. What a palaver it must have been to fill it up every day and then lug it to the lavatory to empty it.

My grandma must have been stitching away as I'm always wearing natty new outfits. By the autumn I'm wearing a tailored coat with a silky lining, a neat little hood and matching buttoned leggings, with small strappy shoes even though I can't walk properly yet.

I had my first birthday. Biddy and Harry gave me a book – not a baby's board book, a proper child's history book, though it had lots of pictures. Biddy wrote in her elaborately neat handwriting: *To our darling little Jacqueline on her first birthday, Love from Mummy and Daddy*.

I don't think I ever *read* my first book, but when I was older, I liked to look at the pictures, especially the ones of Joan of Arc and the little Princes in the Tower. I think my grandma might have made me felt toy animals because there's a photo of me sitting on the rug between Biddy and Harry, playing with a horse with a felt mane and a bug-eyed fawn.

The local paper did a feature on young married couples living in Bath and Biddy and Harry were picked for it. She's wearing a pretty wool dress embroidered with daisies and thick lisle stockings. Harry is wearing a smart suit with a waistcoat, probably his year-old wedding suit, but he's got incongruous old-man plaid slippers on his feet. Did he have to change his shoes the minute he got inside the front door in case he brought mud in?

We look a happy little threesome, sitting relaxed in front of the fire. We *needed* that fire during the winter of 1946/1947. It was so cold that all the pipes froze everywhere. The outside lavatory froze up completely. There was no water, not even cold. Harry had to go up the road with a bucket and wait shivering at the standpipe. Biddy stuck it out for a few weeks, but then she packed a big suitcase for her, a little one for me, dismantled my cot, balanced the lot on my pram, and took us to stay with my grandparents in Kingston.

We stayed on, even when it was spring. Harry lived by himself in Bath until the summer, and then left the Admiralty and managed to get a job in the Civil Service in London, even though he'd left school at fourteen. They looked for a place to rent but half of London had been bombed. There were no flats anywhere, so Harry moved in with my grandparents too.

Which of my books starts with the main girl describing all the beds she's ever slept in, including her baby cot? For a little while they live with her step-gran, though it's a terrible squash – and my poor girl has to share a bed with this grandma.

It's *The Bed and Breakfast Star*.

I had to share it with her. There wasn't room in her bedroom for my campbed, you see, and she said she wasn't having it cluttering up her lounge. She liked it when I stopped cluttering up the place too. She was always wanting to whisk me away to bed early. I was generally still awake when she came in. I used to peep when she took her corset off.

She wasn't so little when those corsets were off. She took up a lot of the bed once she was in it. Sometimes I'd end up clutching the edge, hanging on for dear life. And another thing. She snored.

I love Elsa in *The Bed and Breakfast Star*. She's so kind and cheery, though she does tell really awful old jokes that make you groan! I'm not very good at making up jokes myself, so when I was writing the book, I asked all the children I met in schools and libraries if they knew any good jokes, and then I wrote them down in a little notebook, storing them up for Elsa to use. There were a lot of very funny jokes that were unfortunately far too rude to print in a book!

There used to be several bed and breakfast hotels for the homeless in the road where I lived. I used to chat to some of the children in the sweetshop or the video shop. I knew how awful it must be to live in cramped conditions in a hotel, and many of their mums were very depressed. Still, the children themselves seemed lively and full of fun. I decided to write a book about what it's like to be homeless, but from a child's point of view.

The Bed and Breakfast Star has a happy ending, with Elsa and her family living in the very posh luxury Star Hotel – though I don't know how long they'll be able to stay there!

5

38 Fassett Road

We lived at 38 Fassett Road, Kingston, for the next two years. I was probably the only one of us who liked this arrangement. It was much more peaceful living with Ga and Gongon. These were the silly names I called my grandparents before I could talk clearly and I'm afraid they stuck.

It must have been difficult for my grandparents having a volatile couple and a toddler sharing their living room, cluttering up their kitchen, using the only bathroom and lavatory. It must have been agony for my parents not being able to row and make up in private. They couldn't even be alone together in their own bedroom because I was crammed in there with them in my dropside cot.

I didn't have my own bedroom until I was six years old. I didn't really *need* one when I was little. I didn't have many possessions. I had my cot. I had one drawerful of underwear and jumpers in my mother's chest of drawers. I had one end of her wardrobe for my frocks and pleated skirts and winter coats.

I had my toys too, of course, but there weren't

many of them. It was just after the war and no one had any money. I did royally compared with most little girls. My first doll was bigger than me, hand-made by my Uncle Roy. He was in hospital a long time during the war because his whole jaw was shot away and had to be reconstructed. He passed the time doing occupational therapy, making a huge doll for me, and then later one for *his* newly born daughter Rosemary.

I called my doll Mary Jane. She had an alarmingly nid-noddy head and her arms and legs dangled depressingly but I tried hard to love her. She had brown wool curls, a red felt jacket and a green skirt. You could take her clothes off but then she looked like a giant string of sausages so I generally kept them on. Mary Jane never developed much personality, but I remember being astonished on a rare visit to my uncle and aunt's to find that Rosemary's twin doll had exactly the same staring face and woolly hair and dangling body but wore a yellow jacket and a blue skirt. It was as if I'd found a letter box painted yellow, a lamppost painted blue. She was my first doll, my only doll, and I thought all other rag dolls would be identical.

I was given a new doll the next Christmas. I had a doll every single Christmas throughout my childhood – and a book for my birthday. My next doll was Barbara. She was a real shop-bought doll with a cold hard body and eyes that opened and shut if you tipped her upside down. The first day I owned her I tipped her backwards and forwards until she must have been dizzy, and her eyelids went *click click click* like a little clock. Her eyes were brown and her hair was short and brown and curly, rather like mine. She had a frock with matching knickers and little silky white socks and white plastic shoes that did up with a small plastic bobble.

She was a little girl doll, not a baby, but she had her very own pram. Her composition legs were permanently bent in a spread sitting position so she was very happy to be wheeled about. I pushed the pram around my grandma's back garden and up and down the hallway and in and out of her kitchen.

I had twins the following year, Timmy and Theresa, soft dolls with green checked clothes. Timmy had rompers and Theresa a little dress, again with matching knickers. They had little felt shoes, very soft. The twins were soft all over, but compact – very satisfying after large floppy Mary Jane and hard Barbara, though I tried hard to love all my children equally. Some great-auntie gave me Pandora, a quirky little rag doll with a severe hat and waistcoat and a disconcertingly middle-aged face. My pram was getting crowded by this time.

It was hard to cram all five dolls under the covers.

Then tragedy struck. I was pottering with my pram in the front garden, wheeling my family round and round the pretty crocus patch, when the Maloneys' mad dog came bounding in the front gate. The Maloneys were a very large Irish family, all with carrot-coloured hair and a zest for living. They'd been bombed out and temporarily rehoused opposite my grandparents, causing havoc in the quiet suburban street.

The dog barked furiously and then leaped at my pram. I screamed. Biddy and my grandma came running but they were too late. The dog seized hold of Timmy and ran off with him, shaking and savaging him as if he was a huge rat. He dropped him halfway down the street, tiring of the game. Timmy was brought back scalped, his face chewed to pulp and both arms severed. I wanted to keep and tend him and love him more than ever, but Biddy and Ga said I couldn't possibly play with him now. Poor Timmy was thrown in the dustbin.

I kept my children cooped up indoors for a long time after that. I rode my little green trike in the garden but tensed anxiously whenever I heard the Maloneys' dog barking. But it didn't put me off dogs in general. I longed for a puppy but Ga wasn't any fonder of animals than my mother.

I would always pat any friendly dog I found and

make up imaginary dogs when I played Mothers and Fathers. When I read the Famous Five books at six or seven, I didn't envy George her adventures or even her famous picnics with lashings of ginger beer. I just longed for her dog Timmy. Then one day out at the seaside we came across a very lifelike toy Pekinese in a department store. It was a model of the artist Alfred Munnings's dog Black Knight, VIP. I was told this stood for Very Important Person, which seemed an excessive title for a dog, but I wasn't quibbling. I *longed* for this wonderful toy dog but it was hopelessly expensive. Astonishingly, Biddy fumbled in her white summer handbag for her purse. She bought him!

'Is he for *me*?' I whispered.

'Well, who else would it be for, you soppy ha'p'orth,' said Biddy.

'Is he going to be my birthday present or Christmas present?'

'You might as well have him now,' said Biddy.

'Oh, Mummy, really! You're the best mum in the whole world!'

'Yes, of course I am,' said Biddy, laughing. 'Now, let's hope you stop going on and on about getting a wretched dog. You've got one now!'

I walked out of the shop with him under my arm. He stayed permanently tucked there for weeks. Old ladies stopped me in the street and asked to pat my dog and acted surprised when they found out he wasn't real. I told them shyly that his name was Vip.

At last I was able to write school essays about My Pet. Vip slept in my arms every night. Even when I was a teenager, he slept at the end of my bed by my feet, like one of those little marble dogs on a tomb. I still have him, though my mum had a go at restuffing him and he's never been the same since – he's very fat and lumpy now. Even his sweet expression has changed so that now he looks both dopey and bad-tempered. He obviously didn't take kindly to being restuffed.

I still don't have a real dog because I travel about too much, but when I slow down and stay put, I intend to have not one dog, but two – a retired greyhound called Lola and a little black miniature poodle called Rose.

Which of my characters had a doll called Bluebell – and a fantasy Rottweiler for a pretend pet?

It was Tracy Beaker, of course.

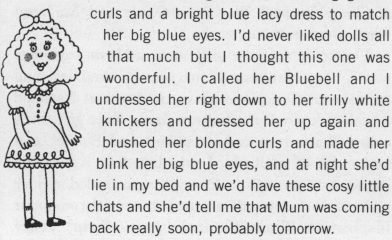

My mum came to see me and she'd bought this doll, a doll almost as big as me, with long golden curls and a bright blue lacy dress to match her big blue eyes. I'd never liked dolls all that much but I thought this one was wonderful. I called her Bluebell and I undressed her right down to her frilly white knickers and dressed her up again and brushed her blonde curls and made her blink her big blue eyes, and at night she'd lie in my bed and we'd have these cosy little chats and she'd tell me that Mum was coming back really soon, probably tomorrow.

Poor Tracy. Someone pokes Bluebell's eyes out and she never feels the same about her afterwards.

I think it's just as well Tracy doesn't *really* have a Rottweiler.

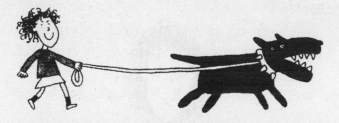

Tracy Beaker is the most popular character I've ever invented. She'd be so thrilled to know she's had a very popular television series, her own magazine, all sorts of Totally Tracy toys and stationery and T-shirts and pyjamas, a touring musical and now *three* books about her, *The Story of Tracy Beaker*, *The Dare Game* and *Starring Tracy Beaker*.

I've often told the silly story of how I got her name. I was lying in my bath one morning, starting to make up Tracy's story in my head as I soaped myself. I knew I wanted my fierce little girl to be called Tracy. It sounded modern and bouncy and had a bit of attitude. I couldn't find a suitable surname to go with it. Everything sounded silly or awkward. I looked around the bathroom for inspiration. Tracy Flannel? Tracy Soap? Tracy Toothbrush? Tracy Tap? Tracy *Toilet*?

I gave up and got on with washing my hair. I don't have a shower, so I just sluice the shampoo off with an old plastic beaker I keep on the edge of the bath. I picked up the beaker. Aha! *Tracy Beaker!*

6

Hilda Ellen

I had two books when I was at Fassett Road. I had my birthday-present history book and now I also had a Margaret Tarrant nursery rhyme book with rather dark colour plates. The children wore bonnets and knickerbockers and boots and fell down hills and got chased by spiders and were whipped soundly and sent to bed. My mum or my dad or my grandma must have read them to me several times because I knew each nursery rhyme by heart.

I can't imagine my grandad reading to me. He was a perfectly sweet, kindly man, though his bushy eyebrows and toothbrush moustache made him look fierce. He put on a pinstripe suit every weekday, with a waistcoat and a gold watch on a fob chain, kept in its own neat pocket, and caught the train from Surbiton. He spent all day at 'business' in London. He was a carpet salesman in Hamptons, a big department store. He was eventually made manager of his department, a very proud day. He always smelled slightly of carpets, as if he secretly rolled himself up in his stock.

He returned home at half past six, listened to *The Archers* on the radio, ate his supper and fell asleep in the armchair, pale hands folded over his waistcoat as if guarding his watch. He gave me a sixpence occasionally or offered me a boiled sweet but that was the extent of our relationship. I don't think I ever sat on his lap. I remember once combing his hair playing hairdressers when I was older, but this was unsatisfactory too, as he had very little hair to comb.

He seemed to have very little of anything, including personality, a nine-to-five man who did nothing with his life – yet he had fought in the reeking muddy trenches in the First World War until he was shot and sent home, badly wounded. Maybe he was happy to embrace a totally peaceful, boring, suburban life – no mud, no bullets, no swearing soldiers, just his little hedge-trimmed semi and his wife, and Phil and Grace Archer and old Walter Gabriel on the radio.

My grandma seemed settled too, perhaps because she'd had such a rackety-packety childhood. I loved curling up by her chair as she sewed, getting her to tell me stories about when-she-was-a-little-girl. These weren't silly Diddle-Diddle-Dumpling See-Saw-Marjorie-Daw stories that didn't make sense, like the rhymes in the Margaret Tarrant book. These were gritty tales of an unwanted, unloved child sent from pillar to post – the sort of stories I'd write myself many years later.

My grandma's mother died of cancer when she was only twenty-seven. Ga, Hilda Ellen, was seven, and her brother Leslie was five. Her father, Papa, was a Jack-the-lad businessman, a fierce, feisty little man up to all sorts of schemes. He palmed his children off on different relatives and got on with his life without them. Leslie was packed off to an uncle, and as far as I know, was never reunited with his sister.

Hilda Ellen was sent to two maiden aunts who were very strict, but they taught her to sew beautifully. She loved dolls. She didn't have a proper big china doll – no one wanted to waste any money on giving her presents – but she scavenged for coppers and sometimes dared save her Sunday school donation, and bought tiny china dolls from the local toyshop. You could get one the size of your thumb for a halfpenny but her hair was only painted in a blob on her head. Penny dolls were the size of your finger and had real silky long hair you could arrange with a miniature brush.

All the dolls were stark naked apart from painted socks and shoes. Hilda Ellen raided her aunts' workbox and made them tiny clothes. At first they were just hastily stitched wrap-around dresses and cloaks, but soon she had the skill to make each doll a set of underwear, even ruffled drawers, and over these they wore embroidered dresses and pinafores and coats with hoods to keep their weeny china ears warm.

The dolls were a demanding bunch and wished for more and more outfits. Hilda Ellen got bolder in her search for material. When the dolls wanted to go to a ball, she crawled to the back of the older auntie's wardrobe and cut a great square out of the back of an old blue silk evening frock. The auntie caught Hilda Ellen twirling her dolls down the staircase, looking like a dancing troupe in their blue silk finery. She recognized the material. She wouldn't have worn that evening frock in a month of Sundays but she was still appalled. Hilda Ellen was sent packing.

Papa had taken up with a new lady by this time and didn't want a daughter getting in the way. Hilda Ellen was sent to relatives who ran a pub in Portsmouth. It was a rough pub, always heaving with sailors, not really a suitable home for a delicate little girl, but Hilda Ellen loved it there.

'I didn't have to stay in my room. Well, I didn't *have* a room. I just had a cot and shared with the bar girls. But every evening I helped in the pub, collecting up the glasses. My uncle would often sit me on the counter and get me to sing a song for all the sailors.'

She was given so many pennies she had a whole drawerful of tiny dolls, and she bought her own scraps of silk and velvet and brocade from the remnant stall at the Saturday market.

Then she was given her own big doll! The hairdressing salon along the road had a china doll in the window with very long golden curls of real hair. She sat there to advertise the hairdressing expertise of Mr Bryan, the owner. Hilda Ellen snipped her own hair every now and then, but she often paused outside the salon window, gazing at the beautiful china doll in her cream silk dress, her golden curls hanging right down to her jointed hips.

Mr Bryan didn't have many clients. He was near retiring age. At Christmas he decided to call it a day and close the business. He donated his doll with the long hair to a local charity which was giving a party for all the poor children of Portsmouth. They tied it to the top of the Christmas tree, like a giant fairy.

Hilda Ellen was at the party. She craned her neck, peering up at the wondrous doll. The Mayor of Portsmouth came in dressed as Father Christmas, his gold chain gleaming under his false beard. He started handing out presents from the tree to every child in the room. Hilda Ellen's heart thumped under her muslin bodice.

Maybe Mr Bryan had seen her peering wistfully in his window and murmured a word in the Mayor's ear. Maybe the Mayor truly *was* Father Christmas. Whatever . . . Hilda Ellen was called out, a young lad was sent scampering up a ladder to the top of the tree, and the beautiful doll was put in Hilda Ellen's arms. She clasped her tight, burying her face in that soft golden hair, quivering with happiness.

She called the doll Mabel and loved her passionately. She made her an entire trousseau of elaborate clothes: a sailor suit with a pleated skirt, a velvet dress with tiny pearl buttons and a crochet collar, a winter coat edged in fur, with a fur-trimmed bonnet and a little fur muff to match.

Hilda Ellen was blissfully happy. She wanted to live in Portsmouth for ever but Papa's lady was now his new wife, with a child on the way. When the baby was born, Papa decided they'd save on a nursemaid and bring Hilda Ellen back to make herself useful. She was old enough, wasn't she – ten or eleven at least?

It was a great pity they'd all forgotten exactly how old she was, even Hilda Ellen herself. She'd had a lot of changes of school but she was bright and loved working hard. She shone especially in needlework classes and art, but she was good at all the academic subjects too. Her teachers thought she was definite scholarship material. She sat the exam without a hint of nerves and passed with flying colours, all set to go to a posh girls' high school, her sights fixed on getting into art school later.

There was just the formality of sending in her birth certificate. When Papa eventually found it at the back of a desk drawer, they had a shock. Hilda Ellen had somehow mislaid a year of her life. She was eleven going on twelve. So that was it. She was too old for the scholarship.

It sounds crazy now. I'm sure someone would ensure that this bright, hard-working girl still got a scholarship somehow. Maybe if her father had pushed harder, they'd have made an exception. But people just shrugged their shoulders and said sorry. Hilda Ellen went and lay on her bed, head in her pillow. I don't know whether she wept. I never saw her cry, not even when she was an old lady in terrible pain. She wasn't one to make a fuss, she just got on with things.

She stayed with Papa and her stepmother. She didn't think much of her. She didn't think much of baby Jack either, or his little sister Barbara, who arrived a year or so later. She bathed them and fed them and sang them to sleep every evening while her stepmother cosied up to Papa. Hilda Ellen had to share the nursery with her half-siblings, but she kept Mabel sitting on a high shelf out of harm's way.

She attended the local elementary school until she was thirteen, but then she had to leave to earn her living. She certainly wasn't going to be a full-time nursery maid. She thought she'd found the ideal job. On a material hunt to the Bon Marché department store in south London she saw they were advertising for attractive young girls to work the newly installed elevators. They were very proud of these beautiful brass lifts, considered very glamorous and state-of-the-art for Edwardian times. They'd already employed a little dark girl and kitted her out in a crimson uniform, to be a special lift girl. Hilda Ellen was little and very fair. The Bon Marché management thought they'd found an excellent contrasting pair.

Hilda Ellen went home full of excitement but Papa was shocked at the idea. He'd not cared what she got up to during her childhood but now she was under his roof she had to behave like a lady. Ladies definitely weren't employed as lift girls. Papa thought they were on a par with chorus girls – or worse.

There was no arguing. Hilda Ellen pressed her lips together so hard her mouth disappeared. Perhaps it made Papa think harder about his daughter and what she should do with the rest of her life. She was good at sewing. She'd made all those fancy outfits for that doll of hers, and a few natty bits and bobs for little Jack and Barbara. Perhaps she ought to be properly trained?

He apprenticed her to a milliner. Hilda Ellen stitched away, pins in her pursed mouth, plaiting straw into hats, like some poor princess in a fairy story.

Then, in 1914, war broke out. Papa went to buy presents for Jack and Barbara at Christmas and found there were hardly any toys in the shops. All the best dolls and toy animals were made in Germany, only we were of course at war with the Germans now. Papa was ever enterprising. Now was the perfect time to start up his own doll factory. He knew nothing about doll-making but that didn't deter him. It should be simple enough. He just needed to take some doll to pieces to see exactly how it was made.

Hilda Ellen came home after a long stint at the milliner's. She went upstairs to free her soft hair from its pins and brush it into a fluffy cloud round her shoulders. She looked up at the shelf to nod at Mabel and her lovely longer tresses. Mabel wasn't there.

Mabel was dismembered in a workroom, cut up like meat on a butcher's block. Even her beautiful blue glass eyes were poked into the hollow of her severed head.

Hilda Ellen met my grandfather, George Alfred, the next year. She was walking arm in arm with a girlfriend over Blackheath, deliberately slowing down as they went past the soldiers' convalescent home, giggling when the poor bandaged boys lounging in deckchairs in the garden called out compliments.

George Alfred took a shine to little blonde Hilda Ellen. He asked her if she'd care to go out with him. She liked the look of this dark handsome soldier with his arm in a sling. She said yes. She'd have said yes if he'd been pug-ugly and bandaged like a mummy. She couldn't wait to leave home.

This is a difficult question! Which of my books is dedicated to my grandma – and can you give me a reason why I chose that book in particular?

Look in the front of *The Suitcase Kid*. It says:

In memory of Hilda Ellen Smeed

There are *several* reasons why I chose this book for my grandma. It's about Andy, who has to move backwards and forwards after her parents split up, living one week with Mum, one week with Dad, never having her own room, her own space, her own *life*. I thought the young Hilda Ellen had a lot in common with Andy.

I also have Andy becoming very close to an elderly couple, Mr and Mrs Peters. Mrs Peters has arthritis but still manages to sew, just like my grandma. Mrs Peters gives Andy her own sewing box for Christmas.

It's got all these little compartments stuffed with threads and needles and a silver thimble and a tape measure that snaps back into place when you touch the button. The compartment tray lifts out and at the bottom are all sorts of materials from her own scrap bag, soft silks and velvets and different cottons with tiny sprigs of flowers and minute checks and pin-head dots, all perfect for making into dresses for Radish. She's got so many little outfits now she wants me to change her all day long so that she can show them all off.

I've made her a dance-frock that covers her paws, a velvet cloak lined with cotton wool fur, even a little sailor-suit with a big white collar and a white cap with special ear-holes.

7

Telling Stories

I once asked my grandma what was the most important thing that had ever happened to her.

'Buying our house,' she said.

I was surprised at the time. It seemed such a sad thing to say. It was such an *ordinary* house too, a suburban semi – two bedrooms and a box room, with no distinguishing features. But now I can see that she didn't necessarily mean the bricks and mortar and all the dark heavy furniture and the dull Axminster carpets. I think she meant she'd got a home at last.

She had a peaceful life living with my grandfather. I never once heard them quarrel. The very worst thing they would call each other was *Fathead*, and that was said in terms of mild irritation, nothing more. They weren't a demonstrative couple at all. I didn't ever see them kiss or cuddle or even hold hands. I knew they slept in the same bed because I was allowed to jump into it when Gongon got up to make their early morning cup of tea.

I'd cuddle up with my sleepy grandma until Gongon came back with the big wooden tray and two green china cups of tea and the biscuit tin. He'd give the tray to Ga and clamber carefully back into bed, and then we'd sit up and they'd sip their tea and we'd all nibble custard creams from the tin. They kept the same tin throughout my childhood, replenishing it from Woolworths' loose biscuits counter every couple of weeks. It was orange and yellow and black, a sunset scene with dark silhouettes of buildings against the evening sky. Every time I go to an antique fair I look for that particular tin design. It must be out there somewhere!

Then my grandpa would go off to the bathroom to shave with his bristle brush and cut-throat razor, going ever so carefully *round* his trim moustache, while my grandma wriggled into her corsets. I wasn't supposed to watch but of course I peeped at her from under the blankets. I was fascinated by this large, prawn-coloured garment, so different from my mother's silky camiknickers and suspender belt. My mum had brassieres too, stitched into two rigid pyramids. She left one at the end of the bed each night, and when my dad was being rude, he'd poke the ends with his finger, denting them. My grandma's corset didn't seem to allow for two bosoms. It compressed my grandma's chest into one large upholstered cushion.

Ga kept her dressmaker's dummy in the little box room with her treadle sewing machine. I'd play games with the dummy and sometimes hug her. She felt *exactly* like my grandma in her corsets.

Cassandra and Rose in one of my favourite books, *I Capture the Castle* by Dodie Smith, pretend that their dressmaker's dummy is a genteel friend called Miss Blossom. Ga's dummy didn't have one personality; she played multiple parts in the theatre of my imagination. One day she'd be a fairy queen, the day after she'd be a mermaid, then she'd be my sister, or a big monkey, or my very special best friend.

I didn't have many real friends when I was at Fassett Road, though there are photos of me playing with various children who came to tea. We are wheeling my pram, sitting on my trike, squatting in my sandpit by the French windows. I am the Persil child, smiling in my dazzling white sunsuit, my white socks, my white sandals. I got told off if I marked my socks or scuffed my shoes or spilled orange squash down my beautifully ironed dress. I didn't have a proper bath every day. This was a once-a-week ordeal with red carbolic soap and lots of scrubbing, and if I whined when the shampoo went in my eyes, I was given a good shake. I had a daily 'wash-down', shivering on the bathroom mat, and my nails were cleaned and clipped until my fingers tingled.

I was a reasonably well-behaved child, though as my mum said, I had my moments. If I was naughty, I was sent upstairs to bed. If I was being really irritating, I got smacked too. Parents smacked their children without any guilt or remorse in those days. It was a perfectly acceptable thing to do. I never got really *hurt*. My mum just gave me a slap on the back of my legs or on my bottom. My grandma gave me a light tap if she caught me with a finger in a pot of her delicious home-made raspberry jam, or picking holes where her kitchen plaster was peeling. My grandpa didn't get involved enough to smack. I asked Biddy if Harry ever smacked me. I was frequently frightened of him, right up to the day he died in his fifties, but I couldn't remember him hitting me.

'He hit you once when you were little, and it worked a treat,' said Biddy. 'You were standing up in your cot one evening, howling and howling, and you simply wouldn't be quiet. I went up to try to get you to lie down and go to sleep. So did Ga. You simply wouldn't see reason. So Harry went up and he gave you an almighty whack and you shut up straight away.'

If I'd done something really bad, I tried to talk myself out of being blamed. I didn't exactly fib. I simply told stories.

'*I* didn't do it,' I'd say, wide-eyed, shaking my head. 'Gwennie did it.'

I'd sigh and shake my head and apologize for

Gwennie's behaviour. Gwennie was one of the imaginary friends who kept me company during the day. Biddy and Ga found this mildly amusing at first but the novelty soon wore off, and I found myself being punished twice over for Gwennie's misdemeanours.

'You must always always always tell the truth, Jac,' Biddy said solemnly. 'You mustn't *ever* tell fibs.'

Try telling that to a storyteller!

Which girl in one of my books always tries *to tell the truth? She lives with her grandparents, just like I did when I was little.*

It's Verity in *The Cat Mummy*.

I try very hard to tell the truth. That's what my name Verity means. You look it up. It's Latin for truth.

I can be as naughty as the next person but I try not to tell lies. However . . . it was getting harder and harder with this Mabel-mummy situation.

The Cat Mummy is a very sad book (though there are lots of funny bits too). Many children write to me to tell me about their pets. They're very special to them. They say: 'Dear Jacqueline, I'm nine years old and I love reading your books and I've got a cat called Tiger and a guinea pig called Dandelion. Tiger is stripy and Dandelion loves *eating* dandelions. Oh, and I've got a mum and a dad. I've got a little brother too and he is a *pest*.'

They nearly always mention their pets *before* their parents and brothers and sisters, as if they're much more important. The sad thing is, pets don't live as long as people. I often get the most touching tear-stained letters, telling me that some beloved hamster or white rat has died.

I decided to write a story about a girl whose old cat dies. She feels terrible and wishes she could preserve her in some way. She's just learned about the Ancient Egyptians at school and it gives her a very very weird idea!

8
Shopping

I loved living as an extended family at Fassett Road. I liked all the little routines of my pre-school life. We would walk into Kingston every day to go shopping. It was a fifteen-minute brisk trot, a twenty-five-minute stroll. Biddy stuck me in my pushchair to save time. It was a pleasant walk, across a little blue bridge over the Hog's Mill stream, down a long quiet street of Victorian houses, some large, some small, past the big green Fairfield, past the library, until we could see the red brick of the Empire Theatre in the middle of town. (I was taken to see *Babes in the Wood* there when I was little and loved it, though I found it puzzling that the boy Babe was a girl and the Old Dame clearly a man.)

Ga had already developed arthritis and could only walk slowly, so we strolled together, peering at everything along the way. We had our favourite houses. She would always pause in front of a pretty double-fronted house with four blossom trees in the garden. '*That*'s my favourite,' she'd say, so of course it was my favourite too.

I live in that house now. My grandma is long dead, but I've hung her photo on the wall – and a replacement china Mabel sits underneath.

Shopping was very different in those days. I loved going to Sainsbury's, but it wasn't a big supermarket with aisles and open shelves and trolleys. The Kingston Sainsbury's then had beautiful mosaic-tiled walls like an oriental boudoir. You queued at the butter counter and watched some white-overalled wizard take the butter and pat it into place with big wooden paddles. You couldn't afford very much butter so you always had margarine too. They were both so hard you had to butter the end of the loaf and then slice it. There wasn't any such thing as ready-sliced bread in packets then.

Then you queued at the cheese counter until another white-garbed lady sliced off the exact amount of cheese for you with a wire and ticked your ration book. You queued at the bacon counter and watched the bacon boy (who always wore a pencil behind his ear) use the scary bacon slicer, cutting your four rashers of best back bacon into wavy ribbons on greaseproof paper. You could queue for a whole *hour* in Sainsbury's and still come out with precious little in your string shopping bag.

Then we'd go to John Quality's on the corner by the market. It was another grocer's, with big sacks of sugar and nuts and dried fruit spread out on the floor, just the right height for me. I was always a very good girl, but Gwennie sometimes darted her hand into a sack and pulled out a dried plum, just like Little Jack Horner in the nursery-rhyme book at home.

Then we'd trail round the market, maybe queuing for plaice or cod or yellow smoked haddock from the fish stall on a Friday, spending a long time haggling at the fruit stall and the veg stall. You could get bananas and oranges now the war was over, but everything was strictly seasonal and none of us had ever even *heard* of exotic things like kiwi fruit or avocado pears or butternut squash. Fruit meant apples and pears, veg meant cabbage and carrots and cauliflower. The frozen pea hadn't even been invented. We didn't have a fridge or freezer anyway.

The only shop I disliked was the butcher's – it smelled of blood. The meat wasn't cut up in neat cellophaned packets, it was festooned all over the place, great red animal corpses hung on hooks in the wall, chickens still in their feathers, rabbits strung in pairs like stiff fur stoles, their little eyes desperately sad.

I shut my own eyes. I breathed shallowly, trying hard not to moan and make a fuss, because if I'd behaved perfectly, I *might* be taken to Woolworths for a treat. I loved Woolworths. It had its own distinctive smell of sweets and biscuits and scent and floor polish. (When I left home and went to live in Scotland at seventeen, I used to go into the Dundee Woolworths just to breathe in that familiar smell.)

I liked the toy counter best. I'd circle it on tiptoe, trying to see all the penny delights: the glass marbles, the shiny red and blue and green notebooks, the spinning tops, the tin whistles, the skipping ropes with striped handles. I always knew what I wanted most. Woolworths sold tiny dolls, though sadly not the beautiful little china dolls of my grandma's childhood. These were moulded pink plastic – little girls with pink plastic hair and pink plastic dresses, little boys with pink plastic shirts and pink plastic trousers, and lots and lots of pink plastic babies in pink plastic pants. The babies came in different sizes. You could get big penny babies alarmingly larger than their halfpenny brothers and sisters.

I was a deeply sexist small girl. I spurned all the pink plastic boys. I bought the girls and the little babies, playing with them for hours when I got home. I sometimes made them a makeshift home of their own in a shoebox. I took them for trips to the seaside in my sandpit. Best of all, I stood on a stool at the kitchen sink and set them swimming in the washing-up basin. They dived off the taps and went boating in a plastic cup and floated with their little plastic toes in the air.

I was very fond of the water myself. I hadn't yet been swimming in a proper pool but we'd had several day trips to Broadstairs and Bognor and Brighton when I'd had a little paddle. Most days in the summer Ga took me for a ten-minute walk to Claremont Gardens, near Surbiton Station, where there was a paddling pool. She stripped me down to my knickers and I ran into the pool and waded happily in and out and round about.

I wasn't supposed to go right under and get my knickers wet, but even if I was careful, the other children often splashed and I got soaked. One time Ga thought my knickers were so sopping wet I'd be better off without them, so she pulled my dress on, whipped my knickers off, and walked home with them clutched in a soggy parcel in her hand. We encountered Mrs Wilton, her next-door neighbour, on the way home.

'Look at this saucepot!' said Ga, twitching up my dress to show my bare bottom.

Then she waved my wet knickers in the air while she and Mrs Wilton laughed their heads off. I was mortified. I was worried Mrs Wilton might think I'd *wet* my knickers and then she'd tell her children, Lesley and Martin, and they'd think me a terrible baby.

I liked the trips to the paddling pool, but the

best treat of all was a walk to Peggy Brown's cake shop in Surbiton. There's a health food shop on the site now, but in the long-ago days of my childhood the only health supplements we had were my free orange juice for vitamin C (delicious) and cod liver oil for vitamins A and D (disgusting) and some black malty treacle in a jar that my grandpa licked off a spoon every day.

Our concept of eating for health was a little skewed too: a fried-egg-and-bacon breakfast was considered the only decent way to start the day so long as you were lucky enough to have the right number of coupons; white bread and dripping was a nutritious savoury snack; coffee was made with boiled full-cream milk and a dash of Camp; and as long as you ate your bread and butter first then you always tucked into a cake at tea time.

Ga made proper cooked meals every day. She rolled her own pastry and made wonderful jam with the berries from the back garden, but I can't remember her baking cakes. On ordinary days we had pink and yellow Battenburg cake or sugary bath buns from the baker's near Kingston market – but once a week we went to Peggy Brown's special cake shop.

They were fancy cakes with marzipan and butter cream and little slithers of glacé cherry or green angelica. They had exotic names: Jap cakes, coconut kisses, butterfly wings. There were tarts with three different jams – raspberry, apricot and greengage, like traffic lights. My favourites were little individual lemon tarts with a twirl of meringue on top.

Excellent as they were, the cakes were only incidental. We went to Peggy Brown's to look at the shop windows. The owner had a vast collection of dolls, from large Victorian china dolls as big as a real child down to tiny plastic dolls not very different from my Woolworths girls.

Each season Peggy Brown did a magnificent display: false snow and a tiny Christmas tree in winter; Easter eggs and fluffy bunnies in the spring; real sand and a painted blue sea in summer; red and gold leaves and little squirrels in autumn. Each season every single doll had a new outfit. They had hoods and mufflers and velvet coats, Easter bonnets and party frocks, swimming costumes and tiny buckets and spades, Fair Isle jumpers with matching berets and miniature wellington boots.

Ga and I gazed and gazed. Ga worked out how Peggy Brown had designed the costume, cut the pattern, sewn the seams. I rose up, strode straight through the glass and squatted amongst the dolls. We made a snowman or stroked the rabbits or paddled in the sea or kicked the crackly autumn leaves until Ga gave me a little tug. I'd back out of the glass into the real world and we'd go home and eat our Peggy Brown cakes for tea.

Which of my books features an entire collection of treasured dolls?

It's *Lizzie Zipmouth*.

Dolls! Old china dolls in cream frocks and pinafores and little button boots, soft plush dolls with rosy cheeks and curls, baby dolls in long white christening robes, lady dolls with tiny umbrellas and high heels, a Japanese doll in a kimono with a weeny fan, dolls in school uniform and swimming costumes and party frocks, great dolls as big as me sitting in real wicker chairs, middle-sized dolls in row after row on shelves, and tiny dolls no bigger than my thumb standing in their own green painted garden beside a doll's house.

I once had a very touching letter from a little girl of about nine. She loved playing with Barbies but a friend had come to tea and thought her a terrible baby because she still played with dolls. She told everyone at school and now my poor girl was getting horribly teased. I wrote back to tell her that I'd played with dolls right throughout my childhood and that I still had several sitting on my windowsills or lolling on spare sofas.

I put lots of dolls in my books, especially in *Lizzie Zipmouth*, where Lizzie and her scary step-great-gran bond over their love of dolls. It's a bonding thing in my family too. Ga loved dolls, Biddy loved dolls – in fact she's got a collection that outnumbers

Great-Gran's. Hundreds of little glass eyes stare at you when you go into her spare room! I've got all kinds of dolls in my house too, and so has my daughter Emma.

BROWNS MILK STOUT

9

Lewisham

We moved when I was nearly four. Jean, one of Biddy's friends, had a brother who rented a small flat in a three-storey house in Lewisham. He was ready to move on now, so Biddy and Harry took his two rooms.

I'm sure they were glad to get their own place. I wasn't as keen. I missed Ga and our daily routines and my treats terribly. It wasn't as if I had a place of *my* own. I still had to share their bedroom. I had my small bed and a rug where I was allowed to line up my dolls, and that was it.

We learned pretty quickly why Jean's brother was so keen to move on. A demented man called Stanley lived on the ground floor. He screamed abuse at his cowed wife. He screamed abuse at us too, and at poor Miss Parker, the retired lady who lived on the top floor. He crouched in his flat, ears cocked, and the moment he heard you coming down the garden path he'd be at his window, purple in the face, screeching.

'Hurry up the steps because of Stanley,' my mum would say when we came back from shopping trips.

She didn't need to tell me twice. I charged up in my Clarks sandals, tripping in my haste.

We couldn't escape him even when we were upstairs in our flat. Stanley would start slamming his own door violently. Not once or twice. Over and over again for a good fifteen minutes, while the whole house shook. Harry was out at work at the Treasury from Monday to Friday. Biddy and I were stuck at home. We went out as much as possible, taking the tram as far as we could afford.

I looked young for my age so Biddy sat me on her lap and pretended I was under three so she didn't have to pay the fare. She let me take a book with me if it was a long journey. I now owned the Margaret Tarrant storybook as well as the nursery rhymes. Margaret Tarrant was very popular in those days and Ga sent me Margaret Tarrant animal postcards every week. I also had *Pookie*, a story about a white rabbit with wings, but all these books were too big and cumbersome to take out. I took a Shelf Animal book instead. They were the same size and format as Beatrix Potter, twee tales about toy animals – Stripy the Zebra, Getup the Giraffe, Woeful the Monkey, Gumpa the Bear and a small, fluffy, teddy-type creature called Little Mut.

I begged Biddy and Harry to read them to me at bed time. Now on the tram I murmured my own versions of the stories as I flipped the pages, looking at the brightly coloured pictures. It looked for all the world as if I was reading. Passengers gazed at me in awe and complimented my mother on my precocity. Biddy smirked, pleased she could take pride in me at last. I usually made her cringe in public. I was still immaculately turned out but I had developed a ferociously needy thumb-sucking habit. I didn't just suck my thumb, I frequently hid my nose in a pocket handkerchief, rubbing the soft cotton with my finger.

'Take that thumb out of your mouth and put that hankie in your pocket! You look tuppence short of a shilling,' Biddy said, again and again.

Sometimes she'd jerk my thumb out impatiently but I stubbornly stuck it straight back. I was missing Ga. Maybe Biddy was too. We were certainly both missing Kingston.

We went up onto Blackheath once, but it seemed too bare and wide and empty compared with the oak woods and red deer of Richmond Park, or the gentle meadows of Home Park, with its flocks of sheep and speckled fallow deer. We went to the Lewisham shops but they weren't a patch on Kingston. There wasn't even one market, whereas we had *three* in Kingston: a big fruit and vegetable market, a little apple and flower market, and on Mondays a huge bustling free-for-all market with ducks and chickens and rabbits, bolts of material, socks and knickers, kiddies' clothes, glittery jewellery, toys, kitchenware and general junk.

Lewisham's big shops didn't compare either. They didn't have a Hides, with wonderful wooden cabinets with labelled drawers, and a money machine that whizzed over your head on a track all round the ceiling like a little runaway train, and then chugged back again with your change. It didn't have Bentalls department store, with its fancy Tudor Rose restaurant where Ga and Gongon took me once for a special treat. Bentalls had a big book department, and toys, and Royal Doulton china ladies, and every season they had a special fashion show, with real mannequins swishing up and down the catwalk. The compère told you their names – Jean and Pam and Suzie and Kay – so you felt as if they were your friends. There was always one older, slightly stouter model, and she got called Mrs Harris. I played in my head that she looked after all the other girls and cooked them their supper at night.

We arrived very late for one fashion show and were stuck right at the back, where I couldn't see a thing. Biddy urged me to burrow forwards, though I felt too shy to barge too far. Then suddenly I was lifted up onto a lovely older girl's lap, where I sat entranced for the rest of the show. She was very fair and very thin, with a silver bangle that slid up and down her delicate arm. She let me try it on and everyone went 'Aaah!' I sensed from the way everyone was staring that she was special.

Biddy was pink with excitement when I was returned to her.

'Do you know who that was? Petula Clark!'

She was a very famous child actress and singer. We listened to her in *Meet the Huggetts* on the radio. She went on to be an internationally acclaimed singer in her adult life. Every time I heard her sing 'Downtown' I'd bore my friends, saying, 'Guess what! I've sat on Petula Clark's lap!'

Which family in one of my books lives in a rented flat above a difficult complaining old lady called Mrs Luft?

It's Marigold and Star and Dolphin in *The Illustrated Mum*.

'What a racket!' Mrs Luft was down at the front door sorting through the post. She seemed to be addressing an invisible audience. 'Do they have to be so noisy on the stairs? Up and down, late at night, first thing in the morning. Some people have no consideration.'

Mrs Luft is a positive saint compared with Stanley! I'm sure she feels Marigold and her girls are the worst neighbours in the world. She'd probably be right too, but I have such a soft spot for Marigold and Star and especially Dolphin.

I got the idea for *The Illustrated Mum* in New York! I was there on holiday with my daughter

Emma. We'd had a wonderful day going round the Metropolitan Museum of Art and lots of shops, and now we were sitting down with an ice cream in Central Park, wiggling our sore feet and watching the world go by.

We watched an attractive arty-looking woman wander past. She had the most amazing unusual decorative tattoos. Two little girls were skipping along beside her, in dressing-up clothes and grown-ups' high-heeled silver sandals.

When they were out of earshot, Emma turned to me, smiling.

'They look like characters in one of your books!' she said.

'Maybe I'll write about them one day,' I said – and I did.

Greetings from SUNNY CLACTON

10

Holidays

We had a proper week's holiday by the seaside the first Lewisham summer. We went to Clacton, staying in a hotel called Waverley Hall. This had been carefully chosen (after much peering through brochures) because it wasn't licensed to sell alcohol. My parents thought people who drank so much as a pre-dinner gin and tonic were rabid alcoholics. Waverley Hall boasted many alternative entertainments: a dance held twice a week, a beetle drive and a talent competition.

We have group photos of Waverley Hall guests for year after year of Clacton holidays. When I peer at those fifties families, all the women well permed and posing earnestly for the camera, the men grinning foolishly in their open-necked sports shirts, I feel the adult me would need several stiff gins to do the hokey cokey in their company – but when I was a child, Waverley Hall seemed as glamorous as Buckingham Palace and the evening's entertainment almost overwhelmingly exciting.

Waverley Hall was managed by a charismatic man called Will Tull who struts through my memory singing, 'Let me en-ter-*tain* you!' Every evening there he was, encouraging this stiff congregation of bank clerks and shop managers and secretaries and teachers to run novelty races and sing 'Ten Green Bottles' and join him in his enthusiastic rendition of 'The Music Man'.

'*I am the Music Man and I can p-l-a-y,*' he'd sing.

We'd all yell, '*What can you play?*'

He'd sing, '*I play the . . . trumpet.*'

Then he'd pretend, oompah-oompah-oompah-ing, and we'd all join in too – my mother who couldn't sing a note in tune, my father who was cripplingly shy and self-conscious in public, both oompah-ing at the tops of their voices.

They took dance nights seriously. My dad wore a proper suit and tie and his black patent dancing shoes and my mum wore a sleeveless flowery chiffon frock with a sweetheart neckline. I wore my best embroidered party frock. So long as I behaved myself, I was allowed to stay up for the dance too. I hadn't been taught to waltz or quickstep but I was good at following if someone steered me around, and sometimes my dad let me stand on his shiny shoes and we'd twirl round the ballroom together, stepping in perfect unison.

Will Tull varied dances, announcing Paul Jones swap-your-partner spots and invitation waltzes and Gay Gordons. There was always a conga at the end of the evening. Every single guest stepped and tapped around the ballroom, through the empty dining room, around the kitchens, out into the gardens, across the tennis courts . . . I think if Will Tull had led us down the road, across the esplanade, over the sands and into the sea, we'd have all followed.

The only entertainment I hated was talent night. My dad sensibly steered well clear of this one. My mum did the one and only recitation she knew by heart, 'The Lion and Albert', with a fake northern accent. This was strange, because she normally detested accents of any sort. She was so worried I'd 'pick up' a Lewisham south London twang and drop my aitches like 'ankies that she started sending me to elocution lessons at *four*. Mercifully, there was no 'How now, brown cow' twaddle. We learned poems instead.

I was the littlest and I had a good memory so it was easy for me to shine. My entire elocution class was entered for a public competition. We chanted an interminably long poem about birds. I was the Yellow Hammer. I had to pipe up, 'A little bit of bread and no cheese!' It went down a treat.

Biddy bought me an A. A. Milne poetry book. (I didn't catch up with Winnie-the-Pooh until much later. When I made friends with a child called Cherry whose parents called her Piglet and her sister Pooh, I didn't understand and thought they were very rude nicknames, if not downright insulting.)

I soon learned a lot of the poems and recited '*What* is the matter with Mary Jane?' at the talent contest the first year at Waverley Hall. I did it complete with ghastly little actions, hands on hips, shaking my head, pulling faces. It was enough to make a sane person vomit but I got loud applause. Biddy was in seventh heaven. She'd always longed for a child like Shirley Temple. She had my wispy hair permed into a grisly approximation of those abundant curls and encouraged me to perform when I was even shyer than my father.

The second Waverley Hall holiday I knew the whole of 'The King's Breakfast' by heart. Oh dear, I've not looked at it since but I've just gone over it in my head and I still know every awful line.

I was scared of performing it in public in front of everyone. I fidgeted nervously throughout our evening meal, going over the poem again and again in my head. I'd got sunburned on the beach and I felt hot and headachy. I gulped down glass after glass of cold water. A big mistake.

Straight after dinner the child performers in the talent contest were herded off to the little room behind the stage in the ballroom. I didn't get a chance to visit the lavatory. I soon realized

I badly needed to go. I was far too shy to tell anyone. I didn't have enough gumption to go off and find a loo myself. I just sat with my legs crossed, praying.

Will Tull had decided to put me on almost at the end because I'd been such a success the year before. I waited and waited and waited, in agony. Then at long long last it was my turn. I shuffled on stage, stood there with clasped hands, head up, chest out, toes slightly turned out, in perfect elocution class stance.

'"The King's Breakfast" by A. A. Milne,' I announced clearly.

A little ripple of amusement and anticipation passed through the audience. I relaxed. An even worse mistake.

> 'The King asked
> The Queen, and
> The Queen asked
> The Dairymaid:
> "Could we have some butter for
> The Royal slice of bread?"'

I declared, as I felt a hot trickle seep down my legs into my snowy white socks.

I didn't stop. I didn't run off stage. I carried on reciting as a puddle spread around my feet. I said the last line, bowed, and then shuffled off in soggy despair.

Biddy came and found me and carted me off to get changed. I wept. She told me that no one had even noticed, which was an obvious lie. I'd seen Will Tull follow me on stage with a *bucket and mop*. Biddy switched tack and said everyone simply felt sorry for me. I'd heard the 'aaahs' myself, so knew this was partly true, but I'd also heard the sniggers from the other children. I was sure they'd make my life hell the next morning at breakfast.

'We have to go *home*! Please please please let's go home,' I begged.

Biddy and Harry scoffed at me.

'But they'll all tease me and laugh at me and call me names,' I howled.

'Don't be so silly. They'll have forgotten all about it by tomorrow,' said Biddy.

This seemed to me nonsense. However, no one stared or whispered when we came down to breakfast the next morning. The children didn't breathe a word about it, not even when we were playing in the ping-pong room without adult supervision. I couldn't understand it. Maybe Will Tull had scurried from room to room and implored everyone to be kind, though this seems highly unlikely. Maybe my mum was right and they really had forgotten. Hadn't even noticed. Whatever.

We carried on our Clacton holiday as usual. We sat on the sands all morning, Biddy and Harry in deckchairs, me cross-legged on a towel, reading or colouring or making sand palaces for my pink plastic children. We had our favourite spot, reasonably near the pier so we could stretch our legs and visit the lavatories, but not so near that the strange, dank, rotting-seaweed, under-the-pier smell tainted our squash and sandwiches.

There were amusement arcades on the pier. I didn't care for them particularly, but Harry loved pinball and Biddy proved surprisingly expert on the crane machines. In one week's holiday she could manoeuvre fifty or sixty toy planes and tiny teddies and Poppit bracelets and packets of jacks and yoyos and pen-and-pencil sets out of those machines, enough for several Christmas stockings for friends' children.

There was a theatre at the end of the pier. I didn't like the journey right along the pier to this theatre. I hated it when the beach finished and the sea began. You could see right through the wooden planks to where the water frothed below. My heart thudded at every step, convinced each plank would splinter and break and I would fall right through.

I cheered up when we got to the theatre and watched the summer season variety acts. I liked the dancers in their bright skimpy outfits, kicking their legs and doing the splits. My parents preferred the stand-up comedians, especially Tony Hancock. When *Hancock's Half Hour* started on the radio, they listened eagerly and shushed me if I dared say a single word.

We went to Clacton year after year. We had a lovely time. Or did we? I always got over-excited that first day and had a bilious attack, throwing up throughout the day and half the night. Biddy would sigh at me as if I was being sick on purpose, but Harry was always surprisingly kind and gentle and would hold my forehead and mop me up afterwards. It's so strange, because when I was bright and bouncy he'd frequently snap at me, saying something so cruel that the words can still make me wince now. I was always tense when he was around. I think Biddy was scared of him too at first. She used to cry a lot, but then she learned to shout back and started pleasing herself.

There was always at least one major row on holiday, often more. They'd hiss terrifying insults at each other in our bedroom and not speak at the breakfast table. My tummy would clench and I'd worry that I might be sick again. I'd see other families laughing and joking and being comfortably silly together and wish we were a happy family like that. But perhaps if I'd looked at *us* another day, Biddy and Harry laughing together, reading me a cartoon story out of the newspaper, I'd have thought *we* were that happy family.

In the days before everyone had ordinary cameras, let alone phone and digital cameras, you used to get special seaside photographers. They'd stand on the esplanade and take your photo and then you could come back the next day and buy it for sixpence or a shilling.

There are two very similar such photos taken the Clacton holiday I was six – but they're so very different if you look closely. The first caught us unawares. It's a cloudy day to match our mood. My father looks ominously sulky in his white windcheater, glaring through his glasses. My mother has her plastic raincoat over her arm and she's clutching me by the wrist in case I dart away. I'm looking solemn in my playsuit and cardigan, holding a minute bucket and spade and a small doll. I am wearing my ugly rubber overshoes for playing in the sand. I do not look a prepossessing child.

Biddy berated Harry and me for spoiling that photograph and insisted we pose properly the next day. The sun is out in the second photograph and we look in a matching sunny mood. Harry's whipped off his severe glasses and is in immaculate tennis whites. Biddy's combed her perm and liberally applied her dark red lipstick. I'm wearing my favourite pink flowery frock with a little white collar and dazzlingly white sandals. I've just been bought a new pixie colouring book so I look very pleased. Biddy is holding my hand fondly. Harry has his arm round her. We look the happiest of families.

This is an easy question. In which of my books does a little girl wet herself on stage?

It's *Double Act*, my book about identical twins Ruby and Garnet.

They are jointly reminiscing about the time they played twin sheep in the school Nativity play. Ruby is being mean, teasing Garnet about it, even though she knows it's her most painful and humiliating secret.

She got so worked up and nervous when we had to perform on stage that she wet herself. On stage. In front of everyone. But it didn't really *matter*. I don't know why she still gets all hot and bothered if I happen to bring it up. It was dead appropriate, actually, because that's what real sheep do all the time. They don't hang around the stable with their back legs crossed, holding it in. They go all over the place. Which is what Garnet did. And everyone thought it was ever so funny. Except Garnet.

I longed for brothers and sisters when I was a child. I particularly wanted a twin sister, someone to play with all the time, someone to whisper to at night, someone to cuddle when Biddy and Harry were yelling.

I can see it could have disadvantages though if you have a very bossy dominant twin like Ruby!

Mummy Daddy Me

11
School

I can't remember my first day at Lee Manor School. I asked my mother if I cried and she said, shrugging, 'Well, all children cry when they start school, don't they?'

I know I cried over my school dinners. I didn't like meat very much and I hated fat. In those days school dinners were mostly fatty mince, stew with large yellow chunks of fat still on the meat, boiled beef and carrots, the fat tinged pink this time, and occasionally stringy roasts with long slender strips of gristle and fat. Fat fat fat. I tried chewing. I tried swallowing whole. I tried spitting it out into my handkerchief.

'Come along, Jacqueline, eat up your dinner and stop being naughty!'

The world where children could choose their own school dinners was far in the future. I tried hard to eat the fat, tears pouring down my face, and then I'd throw up in the smelly lavatories.

The school dinners made their greasy mark upon each day, but I started to learn to read 'cat' and 'hat' and 'mat' and recite the two times table. I chalked pictures – three round blobs with stick arms and legs and smiles across their stomachs and wobbly printing underneath. *Mummy. Daddy. Me.*

I sang *'Daisies are our silver, buttercups our gold'* and *'Jesus bids us shine with a pure clear light'*. I skipped in the school hall in my vest and knickers. I listened avidly at story time, sitting cross-legged, hands on knees, the way we were taught. I made friends with a little girl who had the two things I wanted most in the world: a baby sister and a tiny Yorkshire terrier. I can't remember my friend's name, or her cute sister's, but the dog was called Rags and I loved him, even though he yapped hysterically when I tried to pat him.

I was making good progress at school, but then I got ill. I had measles badly, and then bronchitis, and then, unbelievably, whooping cough, all in the space of six weeks. I can remember those long hot days, coughing until I was sick, and the even longer nights, wide awake and staring into the darkness. I did my best to *stay* awake too, stretching my eyelids wide open, biting my lip, digging my nails into my fingers so that I'd make long ragged hangnails.

I was too scared to sleep because then the nightmares would start. Men would climb right through my bedroom wall and grab at me. They'd pursue me through the streets and chase me on

96

dodgems at the fair. They'd jump out at me as I ran down long corridors. They'd shove me down stairs, throw me out of windows, topple me off towers. I'd fall and fall and fall and then wake up, heart thudding, head pounding, my nightie rucked up round my waist. I'd pull it down and tuck my legs right up inside and wrap my arms round myself and huddle under the covers.

Biddy had told me to say to myself, 'It's only a silly dream' – but the men weren't running after her, they were out to get *me*. I knew they were real, lurking in the wardrobe. Catch me ever tunnelling through to Narnia. I wouldn't dare so much as open the door.

If it was really late and Biddy and Harry had gone to bed, I could clamber in with them. They'd sleepily protest but mostly put up with me. It was much worse if they were in the other room and I was on my own. I'd wait and wait, trying to count my newly learned numbers, and then I'd call out.

I'd always ask for a glass of water. Biddy came a few times and that was wonderful. She'd tell me off, but not seriously. She'd give me my water, turn my pillow over and settle me down again firmly, giving me a quick kiss on the cheek. But nearly always it was Harry. He could be lovely too, gentle and kind and funny. Or he could be cold and impatient and tell me he was sick of this lark. Or he could yell ferociously for no reason. It was so scary not knowing which mood he'd be in. Other little girls could charm their fathers. They could laugh and tease and joke and their fathers would smile at them fondly. I didn't have a clue how to *do* that. I smiled too anxiously, I begged too cravenly, I froze rigid with my thumb forever in my mouth.

However, Harry was very patient with me during the measles-bronchitis-whooping-cough episode. Maybe he should have gone into nursing, though I don't think that was a career option for a man in those days. He rubbed my back, he held my sick bowl, he gave me drinks of water, and if I was awake when he came home from work, he'd read to me.

He read me 'Tuppenny and Squibbit', a cartoon strip in the *Evening Star*, a London newspaper. Tuppenny was a little girl and Squibbit was half a squirrel and half a rabbit. I longed for a pet like Squibbit. When he was in a very good mood, Harry would pretend to be Squibbit and I'd be Tuppenny and feed him nuts. Then Harry would read *my* little cartoon book about Mary Mouse who lived in a doll's house with a dolly family.

I could read the easy Enid Blyton words myself now. I could stagger through my first Noddy book too, though even at five I found the little nodding man and his big-eared buddy highly irritating. Harry introduced me to the Blyton Faraway Tree books. I found these magical in all senses of the word. I was no longer lying hot and itchy and coughing in my narrow little bed. I was wandering through the Enchanted Wood with Jo, Bessie and Fanny, climbing the Faraway Tree, sliding down Moon-Face's slippery-slip slide, sharing toffee-shock sweets with Silky the fairy and her funny walking clock, climbing the little ladder to the land above. I had a snowball fight with snowmen, I battled red goblins, I tumbled over in Rocking Land, and best of all, I went to the Land of Birthdays and ate wishing cake. I was tempted to wish for a fairy outfit like Bessie with real flying wings, but I always plumped for Fanny's wish, a walking talking doll with her own suitcase of clothes.

It can't have been much fun for my father but he read his way through all three Faraway Tree books – and then went on to read me the first few chapters of *David Copperfield*, a mighty literary leap upwards for both of us. I don't know *why* he chose Dickens. He wasn't a man who read the classics himself – he liked Hammond Innes and Ian Fleming. I listened, enthralled. I expect a lot of it went over my head but I still loved this story of young Davey. I was delighted to discover that children in adult novels were much more complex characters than Jo, Bessie and Fanny, with rich inner lives and fears and fancies. I smiled when Davey was with his mother and dear Peggotty, I nibbled my lips raw when his hateful new stepfather was treating him so cruelly, I breathed great sighs of relief, stretching out under the covers, when they went to Yarmouth. *I* got to know all the Peggotty relations and played with Little Emily. I made up further adventures just for Little Emily and me.

My dad never read on into David's adult life. Perhaps he thought I'd lose all grasp of the story. Perhaps I simply got better. It left a deep impression on me though. I still can't read those early chapters without hearing my father's calm quiet voice saying the words – such a *different* voice from when he was in one of his rages.

When I'd stopped whooping, I was still so weak that Biddy had to borrow a baby's pushchair to wheel me around in. I went back to school eventually but it was hard going. I'd missed so many lessons. There are still black holes in my basic knowledge. They'd learned the alphabet when I was away. To this day I find it hard to remember whether 'f' comes before or after 'h', and what about 'o' and 's', and where does 'q' fit in? I have to sing the alphabet song inside my head to work it out.

I missed the rudiments of maths too. I've never

quite *understood* sums. When I'm calculating, I still frequently use my fingers.

Biddy didn't worry that I'd fallen behind at Lee Manor. We were about to move so I'd be going to a brand-new school. We were going to get our own home at last.

*Which sisters have a father as irritable
and unpredictable as Harry?*

It's Prudence and Grace in *Love Lessons*.

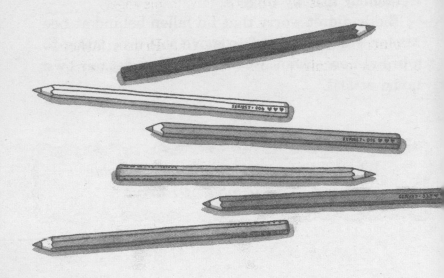

'Oh, Miss Know-It-All! Only you know damn all, even though you think you're so smart. You need to get to grips with maths, even if you're just going to waste your time at art college. Remember that, missy. You thought you could swan off and do your own thing, tell bare-faced lies to your own father, waste everyone's time and money—'

He stopped short, his mouth still working silently though he'd run out of words.

'Bernard? Do calm down – you're getting yourself in such a state. You're making yourself ill!' said Mum, catching hold of his arm.

He brushed her away as if she was some irritating

insect. He focused on me. His face was still purple.
Even his eyes were bloodshot with his rage.

Harry wasn't really a bit like Prue's father –
but they certainly ranted in a similar manner!

12

Cumberland House

My parents had had their name down for a council flat for years. They'd given up on the whole idea when a letter came. Three new six-storey blocks of flats had been built on Kingston Hill. My parents were offered number twelve, on the first floor of the south block.

Cumberland House looks a bit of an eyesore now, three well-worn square blocks with satellite dishes growing out of the brickwork like giant mushrooms. In 1951 they seemed the height of luxury. There was *central heating*! No more huddling over a smoking fire in the living room and freezing to death in the bedroom, having to dress under the eiderdown in winter. There was a fireplace just for show in the living room. We used it as a centrepiece. The Peter Scott print of wild birds hung above it, with our three painted plaster ducks flying alongside.

We had *constant hot water*. This meant we could have a bath every single day. No waiting for the boiler to heat up and carting tin baths around. We could have a bath first thing in the morning or last thing at night. Biddy could wash our clothes whenever she wanted. Well, she didn't ever *want* to wash them, though she did so diligently. She was a feminist long before the word was invented. When I asked her about washing some PT kit one time, she snapped, 'Why should *I* have to wash it?' I said without thinking, 'Well, it's your job, isn't it?'

I wasn't meaning to be cheeky, but Biddy was outraged. It made me rethink the whole concept of what a mum was supposed to do. Jo and Bessie and Fanny's mum cooked and cleaned and washed the clothes – though David Copperfield's mother lay limply on her chaise longue while the servants did the chores. *My* mum, with her smart clothes and her lipsticks and her cigarettes, wasn't anything like *their* mums.

There was a communal laundry room for each block of flats. There were no washing machines, just big sinks in which you scrubbed the clothes using a wash board, and then you squeezed the water out using a big mangle. Biddy seldom fancied carting our clothes downstairs and chatting to the other women. She washed at our kitchen sink, wringing the clothes out fiercely and spreading them out on the dryer. She ironed everything with elaborate care. She even ironed Harry's socks, spreading them out and ironing up to the heel, and then neatly tucking them into paired balls for the airing cupboard.

The best thing of all about Cumberland House was the fact that *it had two bedrooms!* My parents had the biggest bedroom, of course, but I still had a whole room all to myself. I was six years old and I had my own space at last. It wasn't decorated as a little girl's room. I'd read about Ellie's pink and white bedroom in an abridged version of *The Water Babies* and I'd felt as awestruck as sooty Tom, but it didn't occur to me that I could ever have a room like that. We had very little money, and Biddy and Harry weren't the sort of parents who made frilly curtains or wooden furniture.

My bedroom had a built-in wardrobe so I could hang up my favourite dresses in a row: my rainbow party frock; my white dress with the cherry print and little cherry buttons; my blue and green flowery dress with puff sleeves; my pink dress with the fruit pattern and the white collar; my sundress with frills at the shoulders like little wings. There were also the clothes I *didn't* like. I detested my navy pleated skirt, which was stitched onto a white bodice. The pleats stuck out at the front. Biddy was forever telling me to pull my stomach in. I also hated my good Harella coat, fawn with a fancy velvet collar. I was supposed to wear it with a pale brown velour hat. I had to wear both the coat and the hat to my new school and got horribly teased. The boys adopted my velour hat as a new football.

I can't say I blamed them.

I had my own proper big bed, brand new, but I had to make do with my parents' old brown eiderdown. It had a gold-thread pattern and it felt silky to the touch, but it was a hideous colour. I had a brown ottoman too, an ugly piece of furniture from Ga's junk room, hard as a rock to sit on, but the seat lifted up like a lid and I could store all my drawings and paper dolls and notebooks inside, plus all my 'sets'. I had a doctors and nurses set, a red plastic case containing various odd instruments and a toy thermometer and stethoscope. I also had a nurse's apron and cap marked with a red cross. I was therefore the doctor *and* the nurse, so all my dolls got first-class medical attention when they were poorly.

My toys all seemed career-orientated. I also had a bus conductor's set with a dinky little ticket holder and a machine to punch the ticket; a small grocery shop with tiny jars of real sweets and little cardboard boxes labelled Daz and Omo and Persil; and a post office set with a rubber stamp and pretend postage. I politely played with these a few times, but if I wanted to play buses or shops, I found it easier *imagining* it. These little props always reminded me that I was simply playing a game. Still, they were useful when the little girl next door, Suzanne, came in to play with me. It gave us something to *do* together. I liked playing with Sue but if I was truthful, I preferred playing by myself.

I had a second-hand chest of drawers. The drawers all stuck so you had to jiggle them around and tug hard at the handles. Once I pulled a handle right off and got severely told off. It might be an old junk-shop piece of furniture but it was all we had.

I kept jumpers and cardigans in one drawer. Biddy hadn't inherited Ga's sewing skills but she liked to knit. She made me jumper after jumper, using her favourite 'rabbit-ears' stitch. Biddy said they looked 'jazzy', and used very bright contrasting colours. They were tight and itchy, and although they were beautifully knitted, Biddy never quite mastered the knack of stitching the sleeves onto the main garment. I always had odd puckers on my shoulders. Sometimes the sleeves were so tight I held my arms out awkwardly to ease the tension. We didn't wear uniform at Latchmere, my new school. I wished we did.

I kept my Viyella nighties and my vests and knickers and socks and pocket handkerchiefs in the bottom drawer, all jumbled together. Biddy wanted to keep them neatly separate, using the two half drawers at the top, but I wanted these for my special things.

I kept tiny books in the right-hand drawer. I had the little illustrated prayer book that had once been

Biddy's. Ga gave it to me one day. I was surprised. My dad had once been a choirboy – I'd even seen a photo of him in a long gown with a white collar, standing with his brother Roy – but to the best of my knowledge Biddy had only set foot in a church twice: once when she was married and once when I was christened.

It was a beautiful pearly white book and I longed to show it off at school. It had my mum's name neatly written in the front – *Biddy Clibbens* – but in the back I found a pencilled parody of the Lord's Prayer. It was just a silly schoolgirl version, not really blasphemous, changing 'daily bread' to 'daily bath' and that sort of thing, but I got terribly worried. We had a fierce scripture teacher at school, who scrubbed our mouths out with carbolic soap if we said rude words and rapped us on the knuckles if we printed God or Jesus without capital letters. I was sure she'd think my mother would burn to a crisp in Hell if she saw her schoolgirl prank. Biddy found me agonizing over her naughty rhyme.

'You silly little prig!' she said, laughing at me, but she got an eraser and rubbed vigorously until there wasn't a trace of it left, simply to stop me worrying.

I worried a great deal. Biddy didn't seem to worry at all. She'd been bright at school and at eleven had passed her exams to go to the girls' grammar school. Ga was so pleased. She'd lost her chance of a proper education but now her daughter could benefit. Biddy had other ideas though. She didn't take lessons very seriously and got distracted by boys. She was happy to leave school at sixteen.

For various reasons *I* left school at sixteen too. Poor Ga. I wish she could have stayed alive to watch her great-granddaughter Emma grow up – at last a bright, focused child who worked diligently, came top in all her exams and is now a senior academic at Cambridge. *And* she can sew!

I kept Biddy's prayer book – without the Lord's Prayer – with my Mary Mouse series and a whole flock of Flower Fairy books by Cicely Mary Barker. I loved these little books and spent hours poring over the carefully painted pictures, making up stories about all the fairies, gently stroking their long shiny hair, sometimes tickling their bare toes. I never bothered reading the odd little rhymes on the facing pages but I learned all the flower names. The sweet-pea picture of the big sister fairy tenderly adjusting the pink bonnet on her little baby sister was my all-time favourite.

I had two storybooks by Cecily Mary Barker too, stories that I loved, more stirring than the Faraway Tree books, more accessible than *David Copperfield*. *The Lord of the Rushie River* was about a sad little ill-treated child called Susan, desperate for her sailor father to come home. She's carried away by her friend the swan, and of course she's reunited with her father at the end of the story. She's worried about her ragged clothes but the swan snatches her a beautiful rainbow-embroidered dress.

I tried to make friends with the swans on the Thames when Harry took me to feed the ducks, but their beaks seemed very forbidding and I didn't like the way they hissed at me. They certainly didn't look as if they'd take me for a ride on their feathery backs and find me a lovely new dress.

The second book was *Groundsel and Necklaces*, a tender little tale about a child called Jenny who ends up with 365 necklaces, one for every day of the year. I read these stories over and over again. I loved stories about sad, spirited little children going through hard times. I already knew I wanted to write that sort of story myself one day. I cared passionately about dresses and treasured my own rainbow party dress with smocking from C & A. I didn't have any jewellery at all at that age but read the page where the necklaces are described over and over again. I never dreamed that one day I might have a *ring* for – well, not every day, but at least every week of the year.

I had my little books in the right-hand drawer. I kept my crayons and paints and pens and pencils in the left. I didn't have proper *sets*, though in my teens I'd buy myself a beautiful Derwent coloured pencil every week with my pocket money until I had the entire range in every single shade. Meanwhile I kept my mix of crayons in a biscuit tin with a picture of a little girl called Janet on the top.

Janet was a very popular child model in those days, her photo in all the women's magazines. She had wispy hair, big eyes and a soulful expression. She was wearing a seersucker frock on my tin and peering slightly cross-eyed through several branches of apple blossom. I'd have Janet on her tin beside me as I drew and crayoned, and so long as I was out of earshot of my parents, I'd chat to her companionably.

I also had a small Reeves paintbox, though I was never entirely successful when it came to watercolour painting. I could control my crayons and get the colours to stay in the lines, but the paint ran away with me. I'd try to create a fairy princess with hair as black as coal, but the black would run into her pale pink face and she'd end up looking like a coal *miner*. I'd start a beautiful mermaid with long golden curls and a shining tail but the blue sea would splash right over her and dye her hair bright green.

I kept my doll's house and my toy farm on the

top of my chest of drawers. I was never really a country girl and didn't play with my farm very much. Maybe this was just as well, as the little cows and sheep and chickens and turkey were all made of lead, and I was exactly the sort of silly child who might have licked them. The farm stayed undisturbed most days, the cows not milked, the sheep not shorn, the eggs uncollected. I was busy next door, playing with my doll's house.

It wasn't especially elaborate, a two-up, two-down 1930s little number with a scarlet roof and green latticed windows, but it was fully furnished. I especially loved my three-piece suite in jade-green plastic. It gave me great pleasure just holding the little armchair and running my thumb up underneath, feeling the strange insides.

I had a proper family of doll's house dolls, dear little creatures with woollen hair and tiny clothes, but they were made like pipe cleaners, and if you tried to bend them to sit on the sofa or climb up the stairs, a leg might snap off suddenly in an alarming fashion. Sometimes I just played that it was *my* house. I'd stand with the front swinging open, my face almost inside the rooms, and I'd act like Alice and shrink myself small.

I didn't have a proper edition of *Alice in Wonderland* with the Tenniel illustrations. My *Alice* had sugar-sweet coloured pictures that didn't fit the story at all. I also had an abridged *Peter Pan* with Mabel Lucie Attwell illustrations. Both stories confused me, and because I read them consecutively when I was about six, they amalgamated oddly in my head, so that Peter flew round Wonderland and Tinkerbell shook pepper at the Duchess and Alice joined up with Wendy to make a little house for the Lost Boys.

I'd have been perfectly happy left to my own devices playing alone all day in my new bedroom – but I had to go to school.

Who had a very small bedroom at her dad's house, with a chest of drawers half painted silver?

It's Floss in my book *Candyfloss*.

It was not much bigger than a cupboard. There was just room for the bed and an old chest of drawers. Dad had started to paint it with some special silver paint, but it was a very small tin and it ran out before he could cover the last drawer. He'd propped a mirror on top of the chest and I'd laid out my brush-and-comb set and my china ballet dancer and my little cherry-red vase from my dressing table at home. They didn't make the chest look much prettier.

'Dad's going to finish painting the chest when he can find some more silver paint,' I said. 'And he's going to put up bookshelves and we're going to get a new duvet – midnight-blue with silver stars – and I'm going to have those luminous stars stuck on the ceiling *and* one of those glitter balls like you get at dances – and fairy lights!'

I always try hard to describe the bedrooms of all my girls. I feel so lucky that I can choose whatever style of bedroom I like now. It's got a very big wardrobe along one wall, and when you open the doors, a little light goes on. I've got a pink velvet Victorian chaise longue by the window. There are specially built bookshelves, a Venetian glass dressing table and big mirrors, and a special shrine of pretty Madonnas and angels and a heart-shaped gold sacred relic with a secret message inside. My fashion mannequin Crystal stands in the corner wearing a beaded black evening frock. She has matching black velvet ribbons in her long fair hair. There's a picture of a doll my daughter Emma drew when she was twelve on the wall. There are more dolls sitting smiling in odd corners and two droopy knitted animals, one a dog and one an elephant. They are *very* like Dimble and Ellarina in *Candyfloss*.

Dimble

Ellerina

Ann

Michael

13

Latchmere Infants

It's always a bit of an ordeal starting at a new school, especially in the middle of the term. Everyone else has had a chance to make friends. You're the new girl, the odd one out, the one with the weird clothes, the one who doesn't know the way to the toilets, the one who doesn't know where to sit at dinner time.

I had to stay for school dinners at Latchmere because it was too far away to walk home at lunch time. Biddy didn't want me to go to the nearest school at Kingsnympton, the neighbouring council estate. She got it into her head that the Kingston school *furthest* from our flats was the best one and somehow or other wangled me a place there.

It was a problem getting me to school. We didn't have a car. It would be another ten years before we could afford one. The tandem had fallen to bits. Both my parents now had bikes. Harry cycled twelve miles up to London on his. Biddy attempted the couple of miles to my school with me perched precariously on the back. To my shame I couldn't ride a bike myself. Harry had tried to show me but I didn't seem to have any idea how to steer and kept falling off with a clunk so he got irritated and gave up on me.

I was quite a small child but I was really too big to squat on the back of a bike, so after a few weeks Biddy trusted me to walk to school and back by myself.

'You must look both ways every time you cross a road, do you hear me?' said Biddy.

'Yes, Mummy.'

'There's a traffic lady at the Park Road crossroads – she'll show you across.'

'Yes, Mummy.'

'You do know the way by now, don't you, Jac?'

'Yes, Mummy.'

'And you won't ever talk to any strange men?'

'Yes, Mummy.'

'*What?*'

'I mean, no, Mummy.'

'And absolutely *no daydreaming*!'

'Yes, Mummy. No, Mummy,' I said. No daydreaming! It was as if she was telling me to stop breathing.

It wasn't that unusual to let young children walk to school by themselves in those days. Children in the country would think nothing of walking three or four miles. I liked my half-hour's walk through the quiet suburban streets. I'd make up stories inside my head or talk to imaginary friends. If people started looking at me strangely, I'd realize

I was muttering to myself. I soon perfected a mask expression while inside I was up to all sorts. I already knew I wanted to be a writer. Sometimes I'd pretend to be grown up and a famous author and I'd interview myself. Nowadays it still feels faintly unreal when I'm being interviewed, as if I'm still making it up.

The walk *back* from school was much more worrying. I met up with more children wandering home from their own schools. They were mostly in little gangs. I was on my own. There was one boy in particular who really scared me. He went to the school my mother had spurned. Francis wasn't a rough boy, quite the contrary – he came from a wealthy bohemian family who lived in a huge Victorian house at the bottom of Kingston Hill. Biddy knew the family and turned her nose up at them because the children had tousled hair and colourful crumpled clothes and scuffed sandals. I liked the way they looked, especially Rachel, the thin little girl with a gentle face and spindly plaits.

Francis wasn't gentle though. He glared at me every day, clenching his fists. I scurried out of his way as quickly as possible. Sometimes he'd chase after me, thumping me on my back if he got close enough. I'd arrive home shaky and tearful. I didn't want to tell Biddy. She might go to find Francis and tell him off, and any fool knew that that would make him *really* out to get me.

I pretended I had a stomach ache instead. I had a dodgy stomach at the best of times, and had bad bilious attacks every couple of months, so Biddy took me at my word. Sometimes she'd let me climb on her lap and she'd rub my tummy and I'd feel a lot better – though I had nightmares about Francis at night.

Then one day Francis caught hold of me, said a surprisingly rude word, and then punched me hard in the tummy. I had a *real* stomach ache now. It hurt a lot. My eyes watered but I was determined not to cry in front of him. I just stood there, staring straight back at him. He didn't punch me again. He ducked his head and shuffled off. Rachel looked at me anxiously, her face white. She looked as if she was trying not to cry too.

The next day they were standing waiting for me on the corner. I felt sick with fear, but as I got nearer, I saw Francis wasn't glaring. Rachel was smiling timidly. She held out a crumpled bag of home-made fudge.

'These are for you,' she said.

I took the bag. I had a piece of fudge. I offered the bag back to them. They took a piece too. We stood, teeth clamped shut with fudge. Then we swallowed and nodded goodbye. They went down the hill, I went up the hill. We weren't exactly friends now, but we were no longer enemies.

Francis never punched me again.

I found it hard to make school friends the first few days at Latchmere. I wandered around the playground by myself and crept inside the main door and leaned against the radiators, breathing shallowly because the whole corridor smelled of sour milk. We were all given a small bottle of milk each morning. I hated milk, but you had to drink it right down to the bottom or else you got into serious trouble and were lectured about the starving children in Africa. Then the milk monitor collected all the silver tops up and stored them in huge sacks in a cupboard. They stayed there for months before anyone came to collect them.

The head teacher's office was nearby, and the secretaries' office too. There were two secretaries, the Misses Crow, a pair of stout sisters. They both had hearts of gold, but one was sharp and one was sweet and you knew exactly which one to make for if you'd fallen over and needed a bandage.

Miss Stanbridge, the head, was another stout spinster. She bustled past once or twice while I was drooping by the radiator, my expression probably as sour as the milk. Children weren't supposed to be indoors at play times but she didn't chase me outside. She patted me on the head in a kindly fashion, as if I was a little stray dog, and then marched off purposefully in her great black lace-ups.

My form teacher was *lovely*, dear Mrs Horsley. She wore hand-crocheted jumpers and dirndl skirts and was passionate about country dancing. She was a brilliant storyteller and very kind to all the children in her class, though some of the naughtier boys got a light slap on the backs of their legs if they fidgeted or argued. All teachers hit children then. If you were really really bad, you got the cane in front of everyone, but this rarely happened, especially in the Infants.

Mrs Horsley saw I needed to make friends. I think she had a quiet word with two girls in my class, Hilary and Jane, because they decided to take me under their wing. This was very kind of them but I found them a little oppressive. They were tall, gangly, bespectacled girls, very earnest and upright. They played Mothers and Fathers and wanted me to be the baby. They'd whisper to me in their own voices to be naughty, and then they'd sigh and suck their teeth and go '*Bad* Baby!' and act putting me to bed in disgrace.

This got incredibly boring play time after play time. But then one of the boys started playing with us too – Michael, my first boyfriend. He was a cheery boy with slicked-down hair, rosy cheeks and a big smile. His mother dressed him in sensible long corduroy trousers in the winter. Most of the boys then wore ugly grey short trousers that ended an inch or so above their scabby knees. Sometimes their horrible baggy white underpants showed *below* their trouser hems, a total turn-off. Michael had much more style. I liked him – and he seemed to like me.

'What are you girls playing?' he said, circling us with interest.

'We're playing Mothers and Fathers,' said Jane. 'I'm the mother.'

'Then I'll be the father,' said Michael.

'You can't be. *I'm* the father. I'm tallest,' said Hilary.

'Maybe you can be another baby, like Jacky,' said Jane.

'I don't want to be a baby,' said Michael. 'I'll be a monkey, OK?'

He made screechy monkey noises, waddling around and scratching himself.

I giggled.

'You're Micky the Monkey,' I said. 'You're *my* monkey.'

Mothers and Fathers became much more interesting after that. Sometimes we gave Hilary and Jane the slip and played Baby and Monkey games by ourselves.

It was great having a boyfriend. I didn't really have a proper girlfriend for a while. I knew who I liked the most: Ann, a beautiful child with big brown eyes and long curly hair. She was the youngest of four and had that glossy confidence that comes when you're the family favourite. She wore very frilly white knickers that showed beneath her short flouncy frocks whenever she twirled round. Any other girl would have been teased unmercifully about such fancy underwear, but no one ever picked on Ann. She went to ballet classes and sometimes wore her angora ballet bolero to school.

I wanted an angora bolero too, but Biddy wouldn't knit me one because she said the fluff got everywhere and made a mess. I longed to do ballet, but Biddy was against that idea too. She said she'd have to make costumes for me and she didn't have the time or the patience. Ga's hands were twisted with arthritis now and she couldn't take on any costume-making either.

At the end of the first term at Latchmere there was a Christmas concert. Ann wore a white ballet frock with a real sticking-out skirt, and white ballet shoes and a white satin ribbon tying up her ponytail. She did a snowflake dance without one wobble, the star of the show.

I was proud of her, and a little wistful, but I didn't feel jealous. The only time I felt a real stab of envy was a couple of years later in the Juniors when our teacher decided to give out prizes at the end of term.

There were four prizes, one for English, one for arithmetic, one for handicraft and one for sport. I knew I had no chance winning a sport prize. I was the child picked last for any team because I couldn't ever catch a ball. (I was extremely short-sighted but this wasn't discovered until I was ten, so maybe I simply couldn't *see* the ball.) I certainly wouldn't win a handicraft prize because my cross-stitch purses unravelled and my raffia baskets keeled over lopsidedly. I was a hopeless candidate for arithmetic because I couldn't add up or subtract accurately and was a total duffer when it came to problems. *However*, I was good at English. Very good. I wrote longer stories than anyone else. I was good at reading aloud. I was often picked to read a story to the class if the teacher was called away from the classroom.

I so hoped I'd get chosen for the English prize. I didn't get it. Ann did. It was a book, *The Adventures of the Wishing-Chair* by Enid Blyton. I wished wished wished I'd won that book.

I was almost Ann's best friend at that time. We played pretend games together at lunch time, wonderful rich imaginary adventures. Our favourite was playing that we had a tree house right at the top of a huge oak. It took several minutes of energetic 'climbing' before we were safe in our house each play time. That tree stood so tall and sturdy in my imagination that I actually looked

127

for it in the playground when my daughter started going to Latchmere herself years later.

I furnished our imaginary tree house lavishly. We had a library and an art alcove and a tray for our pretend picnics. Ann went along with this, suggesting stuff herself. It was such a joy playing with someone who could invent too. I still fancied myself as the *chief* instigator of our imaginary games though. I was the girl with the vivid imagination, the girl who was always scribbling stories, the girl who always had her head in a book, the girl who was best at English.

But now Ann was that girl, not me.

I went up to Ann and managed to say, 'Well done!' I asked if I could have a look at her book. She showed it to me proudly. We both stroked the nameplate stuck in the front with the word *Prize* embossed in italic letters and then Ann's name written in bright blue ink.

Ann grinned, still very excited, but a little embarrassed too.

'Clever me!' she said.

She said it lightly, sending herself up. I knew she wasn't being *serious*. But when I told Biddy and Harry about the prize that Ann had won, I twisted the tale a little.

'So the teacher picked Ann instead of you?' said Biddy.

'Yes.'

'I suppose she was ever so pleased?'

'Oh yes, she kept going, *Clever me, clever me.*'

'What a nasty little show-off!' said Biddy.

'Clever me' became a catchphrase in our family after that. I always felt a stab of guilt, because I knew I'd been unfair to Ann.

In one of my books the main girl dreads walking home from school by herself because three girls tease her very spitefully.
Which book is it?

It's *Bad Girls* and it's poor Mandy who's getting picked on.

They were going to get me.

I saw them the moment I turned the corner. They were halfway down, waiting near the bus stop. Melanie, Sarah and Kim. Kim, the worst one of all.

I didn't know what to do. I took a step forward, my sandal sticking to the pavement.

They were nudging each other. They'd spotted me.

I couldn't see that far, even with my glasses, but I knew Kim would have that great big smile on her face.

I stood still. I looked over my shoulder. Perhaps I could run back to school? I'd hung around for ages already. Maybe they'd locked the playground gates? But perhaps one of the teachers would still be there? I could pretend I had a stomach ache or something and then maybe I'd get a lift in their car?

I'm very glad I didn't encounter a girl like Kim at Latchmere. Goodness knows how I'd have dealt with her. It's so horrible when you're being bullied. I wanted to write about that particularly mean name-calling teasing that girls are so good at. I've had so many moving letters since from children who have experienced something similar. I'm always so touched if they feel *Bad Girls* has helped them cope.

14

Hospital

I wasn't a particularly robust child. I had my famous bilious attacks, brought on by excitement, anxiety, fatty meat, whatever. Biddy was brisk on such occasions, perhaps thinking I was sick out of sheer cussedness.

'You always pick your moments!' she said, exasperated.

Certainly I chose the only time they left me with Miss Parker at Lewisham to throw up over myself, my bed, the carpet and most of poor Miss Parker. I was frequently sick the first night of a holiday. I was once sick the last two days of a foreign holiday on a coach driving all the way back from the Costa Brava. It was hell for me throwing up repeatedly into carrier bags. It must have been pretty terrible for my fellow passengers too.

Most children are sick once or twice and that's it. I was a little drama queen, being sick at least twenty times over twenty-four hours. I'd not be able to eat or do anything but lie on a sofa with a book sipping Lucozade the next day.

I also had head colds that dragged on for weeks.

I'd sniffle and snort unattractively and then start coughing like a sea-lion. Biddy's remedy was Vick, a smelly menthol ointment in a dark blue jar. She ladled it onto my chest so that my vests and nighties reeked of it, and worst of all, she rubbed it all round my sore nose, even *up* it, so that my eyes streamed. It felt revolting and it meant I couldn't snuffle into my cuddle hankie at night. I couldn't even suck my thumb: my nose was so sealed with Vick and snot that I had to breathe through my mouth.

I'd just be getting better, only coughing when I ran fast, when I'd start to feel that ominous prickling in my nose and the whole cycle would start all over.

Biddy took me to the doctor. He peered down my throat.

'Good God, she's got tonsils the size of plums! We'll whip them out – and her adenoids too – then she'll be right as rain.'

It was the fashion to remove children's tonsils in those days. You didn't argue about it. I was booked in at Kingston hospital for a week. Biddy was to take me there, just five minutes walk down Kingston Hill. She was told when to come and collect me, but there was to be no visiting at all during the week.

'We find it unsettles the children if they have visits from their parents,' the matron said firmly.

134

You *certainly* didn't argue with matrons. It seems so sad now that little children were delivered into this scary place, dragged off by strangers to have bits snipped out of them, and then left alone without a cuddle for days. At least I was six, old enough to understand what was going on.

It was quite exciting at first, almost like Christmas or a holiday. Biddy bought me a new Viyella nightie, white with little roses, and because she knew it was pointless trying to part me from my cuddle hankie, she bought me a new snow-white cotton handkerchief specially for the hospital.

She also bought me a brand-new doll. I'd only ever had dolls for Christmas or birthday before so I couldn't believe my luck. She was a beautiful blonde doll with silky plaits and a soft smiley face. She had a red checked frock, white socks and red shoes. I knew at once she had to be called Rosalind.

My favourite children's book at that time was a wonderfully imaginative fantasy story called *Adventures with Rosalind* by Charlotte Austen. It was about a little boy called Kenneth who was given an amazing picture book with a blonde little girl on the front. She steps out of the picture and takes Kenneth on many magical adventures in different lands. Rosalind was a courageous and cheerful little girl, an ideal friend for adventures. I hoped my Rosalind doll would be the perfect companion for me during my big hospital adventure.

I was in a ward with ten or twelve other children. It was comforting because we were all in this new weird scary world together. I chatted shyly with Muriel, the little girl in the next bed, and let her hold and admire Rosalind. We pulled faces at each other when we had our first trayful of hospital food. We giggled at the antics of the boys in the beds opposite.

It was the nights that were the worst. The ward seemed to grow enormously. It was so dark I couldn't even see my hand in front of my face. There was a little pool of light right up at one end where the night nurse sat at her desk, but there was no way of telling whether she'd be cross or not if she knew I was awake.

I mislaid my new cuddle hankie. The night nurse must have heard me scrabbling around feeling for it. She stood up and walked down the dark ward towards me, her sensible shoes squeaking on the polished floor. I lay still, my heart thudding. She came and shone her torch right in my face but I squeezed my eyes shut, huddled in a ball, pretending to be fast asleep. She hovered over me, but eventually turned and squeaked back down the ward again. I didn't dare carry on searching for my hankie. I clutched Rosalind tight instead and rubbed my nose against her checked skirt.

I wasn't allowed any breakfast the day of my operation. I wasn't even allowed to keep my new Viyella nightie on. I had to wear a strange operation gown, which was only *half* a nightie, with no proper back to it whatsoever, so that my bottom showed if I turned round. I was worried I might need to go to the toilet. I didn't want the boys laughing at me.

I was put on a trolley and given a ride to the operating theatre. I'd hoped Rosalind might be allowed to go with me, but she was left behind on my bed. I tried to imagine she was running after me, jumping up onto the trolley, swinging her legs and laughing. Then we were in this new eerie room full of alien beings in masks and gowns. One of them held me down while another put an evil-smelling rubber mask over my face. I struggled and they told me to calm down like a good sensible girl and start counting, one, two, three . . . It seemed the maddest time in the world to start an arithmetic lesson but I obediently mumbled, 'Four, five, six . . .'

And then I was asleep, and when I woke up, I was back in my bed with Rosalind tucked up beside me, and a raw pain at the back of my throat.

They let each child have ice cream for the first meal after their operation. Ice cream was an enormous treat then. You had ice cream with jelly at birthday parties and you *might* be allowed an ice-cream cone once or twice on your summer holiday, but that was your lot. The hospital ice cream was meagre, a slither of Wall's vanilla, but I swallowed it down eagerly, in spite of the pain.

I had a little parcel from home too. Biddy might not be allowed to see me but she sent me a Margaret Tarrant card every morning, and there was a present too, a little book of *Toy Tales* with big printing and lots of pictures. It was a bit babyish when I could cope with hundreds of pages of *Adventures with Rosalind*, but I knew it was the thought that counted. I was surprised that none of the other children got presents or cards or letters. Everyone thought it must be my birthday. They said I was very lucky and my mum and dad must love me very much.

I don't think any of my fictional girls has to have her tonsils out in my books. However, there are a few hospital scenes, some very dramatic and sad. There are also more routine visits. Which of my characters ends up in hospital with a broken arm?

I wonder if you picked Mandy from *Bad Girls*? She *does* hurt her arm and end up in hospital, but it's just a bad sprain. But Em in *Clean Break* breaks her arm running after her beloved stepfather.

'Em, darling! It's all right, I'm here. Does your arm hurt really badly?' said Dad. 'The nurse has just come, pet, they're ready to plaster you up.'

I clung to Dad, scared that it might be very painful. It *did* hurt when they gently but firmly straightened my arm out.

'There we go. We'll have you right as rain in no time,' said the young doctor, smiling at me. 'There's no complications. It's a nice clean break.'

I winced at those two words.

People often ask me if any of the characters in my books are real. Mostly I make it all up, but just occasionally it's fun to write about someone I really know. I've always said I don't put myself in my books but the novelist Jenna Williams in *Clean Break* is very similar to me. Nick's drawn her looking exactly like me too – apart from one tiny detail. I wonder if anyone can spot what it is?

15
Pretend Friends

Junior school was very different from the Infants. I was still at Latchmere, in an adjacent but identical red-brick building, the classrooms built round a quadrangle of grass. They were mostly the same children in my class but somehow *I* wasn't the same. I wasn't little Jacky-no-friends, the odd girl. I was suddenly inexplicably popular, with the girls, with the boys, even with the teachers.

I wasn't the new girl any more. She was a girl called Cherry, an exotic name in those days of Susans and Elizabeths and Janes. She was nicknamed Cherry Blossom Boot Polish and mildly teased. We became friendly because she lived a few streets away and we walked to school together.

I was sad to miss out on my imaginary conversations on the way to school, but it was companionable having Cherry to walk back home with. We'd take our time. We'd run up the old air-raid shelter in Park Road and slide right down. We'd climb little trees on the bombsite and walk along the planks crossing the trenches where new houses were being built. We'd visit the sweetshop on the way home and buy sherbet fountains and gob stoppers and my favourite flying saucers, cheap pastel papery sweets that exploded in your mouth into sharp lemony powder.

I'd occasionally go home with Cherry. Her mother was sometimes out, as she worked as a hospital almoner. They had a big piano in the living room. The whole family was musical. Cherry played the recorder and the violin. Her parents were keen amateur Gilbert and Sullivan performers.

'Gilbert and Sullivan!' said Biddy, sniffing.

She had a job now too, but it was just part time in a cake shop. Cherry's mum tried to be friendly with my mum, but Biddy wasn't having any. She felt they put on airs and considered themselves a cut above us. I wasn't allowed to invite Cherry back. I wasn't allowed to have *anyone* in to play, not unless Biddy was there. She didn't get home till quarter to six now, but I had a key to let myself in.

Lots of the children in my class had similar keys. They wore them on strings round their necks under their vests. People called them latchkey kids. I thought *I* was a latchkey kid but Biddy soon put me right.

'*You're* not a latchkey kid! As if I'd let you go out with a grubby piece of string round your neck! You have a proper real leather shoulder purse for *your* key!'

I had to wear the purse slung across my chest. It banged against my hip when I ran and it was always a worry when I had to take it off for PT but I had to put up with it.

I didn't mind letting myself in at all, though there was always an anxious moment reaching and trying to turn the key in the stiff lock, jiggling it this way and that before it would turn. But then I was in and the flat was mine. It wasn't empty. It was full of my imaginary friends.

I wasn't allowed to cook anything on the stove in case I burned myself, but I could help myself to bread and jam or chocolate biscuits or a hunk of cheese and a tomato – sometimes all three snacks if I was particularly starving. Then I was free to play with my friends. Sometimes they were book friends. I had a new favourite book now, *Nancy and Plum* by Betty MacDonald. Nancy was a shy, dreamy girl of ten with long red plaits, Plum was a bold, adventurous little girl of eight with stubby fair plaits. They were orphans, badly treated by horrible Mrs Monday, but they ran away and were eventually adopted by a gentle kindly farmer and his wife.

I read *Nancy and Plum* over and over again. I loved the parts where they imagined elaborate dolls for their Christmas presents or discussed their favourite books with the library lady. Nancy and Plum became my secret best friends and we played together all over the flat. Whenever I went on a bus or a coach ride, Nancy and Plum came too. They weren't cramped up on the bus with me, they ran along outside, jumping over hedges, running across roofs, leaping over rivers, always keeping up with me.

When Nancy and Plum were having a well-earned rest, I'd play with some of my *own* characters. I didn't always make them up entirely. I had a gift book of poetry called *A Book of the Seasons* with Eve Garnett illustrations. I thought her wispy-haired, delicate little children quite wonderful. I'd trace them carefully, talking to each child, giving her a name, encouraging her to talk back to me. There were three children standing in a country churchyard who were my particular favourites, especially the biggest girl with long hair, but I also loved a little girl with untidy short hair and a checked frock and plimsolls, sitting in a gutter by the gasworks.

Eve Garnett drew her children in so many different settings. I loved the drawings of children in window seats. This seemed a delightful idea, though I'd have got vertigo if I'd tried to perch on a seat in our living-room window, looking down on the very busy main road outside. I loved the Garnett bedrooms too, especially the little truckle beds with patchwork quilts. I copied these quilts for my own pictures and carefully coloured in each tiny patch.

I'd sometimes play with my dolls, my big dolls or my little doll's house dolls – but perhaps the best games of all were with my paper dolls. I don't mean the conventional dolls you buy in a book, with dresses with little white tags for you to cut out. I *had* several books like that: Woolworths sold several sorts – Baby Peggy and Little Betsy and Dolly Dimples. I scissored my fingers raw snipping out their little frocks and hats and dinky handbags and tiny toy teddies, but once every little outfit was cut out, white tags intact, I didn't really fancy *playing* with them. I could dress them up in each natty outfit, but if I tried to walk them along the carpet or skate them across the kitchen lino, their clothes fell off all over the place. Besides, they all seemed too young and sweet and simpering for any of *my* games.

My favourite paper dolls came out of fashion books. In those days many women made their own clothes, not just my grandma. Every department store had a big haberdashery and material department, with a table where you could consult fashion pattern catalogues – Style, Butterick, Simplicity and Vogue. At the end of every season each big hefty book was replaced with an updated version but you could buy the old catalogues for sixpence. Vogue cost a shilling because their designs were more stylish, but I didn't like them because their ladies weren't drawn very realistically, and they looked too posh and haughty.

I loved the Style fashion books. Their ladies were wonderfully drawn and individualized, with elaborate hairstyles and intelligent expressions. They were usually drawn separately, with their arms and legs well-displayed. It was highly irritating finding a perfect paper lady with half her arm hidden behind a paper friend. She'd have to suffer a terrible amputation when I cut her out.

I cut out incredibly carefully, snipping out any white space showing through a bent elbow, gently guiding my sharp scissors around each long curl, every outspread finger, both elegant high heels.

I'd invent their personalities as I cut out each lady. It was such an absorbing ritual I was lost to the world. I remember one day in the summer holidays, when Biddy was out at work and Harry was *off* work for some reason, sitting at the living-room table with his horse-racing form books and his *Sporting Life*, working out which bets he was going to put on. He seemed as absorbed in his world as I was in mine. I forgot all about him until he suddenly shouted, 'For Christ's sake, do you have to keep snip-snip-snipping?'

I jumped so violently I nearly snipped straight through my finger. I cut out my paper ladies in my bedroom after that, even when I was alone in the flat. I spread each lady out on my carpet. I cut out girls too, especially the ones with long hair, though plaits were an exceptionally fiddly job. I seldom paired them up as mothers and daughters. They were simply big girls and little girls, living in orphanages or hostels or my own kind of invented commune. There would be a couple of men too, but they were usually rather silly-looking specimens in striped pyjamas. No one sewed men's suits from scratch, not even my grandma, so you only got nightclothes and the occasional comical underwear. I certainly didn't want any grinning goofy fools in white underpants down to their knees and socks with suspenders hanging round *my* ladies.

I didn't bother with the boys either, though there were more of them in short trousers. I did have a soft spot for the babies though, and cut out the prettiest. Then I could spend hours at a time whispering my games. My favourite of all my paper girls was a bold, long-haired lady called Carola, in a lacy black bra and a half-slip. She was a naughty girl and got up to all sorts of adventures. I'd carry her everywhere with me, tucking her carefully inside my book.

Which of my characters has paper girls with special flower names?

It's April in *Dustbin Baby*.

I carefully cut out long lanky models with skinny arms and legs, my tongue sticking out as I rounded each spiky wrist and bony ankle, occasionally performing unwitting amputations as I went.

Sylvia found me an old exercise book and a stick of Pritt but I didn't want to make a scrapbook. I wanted to keep my paper girls free. They weren't called Naomi and Kate and Elle and Natasha. They were my girls now, so I called them Rose and Violet and Daffodil and Bluebell.

I seem overly fond of the name Bluebell. It's also the name of Tracy Beaker's doll and Dixie's toy budgerigar. Sorry I keep repeating myself!

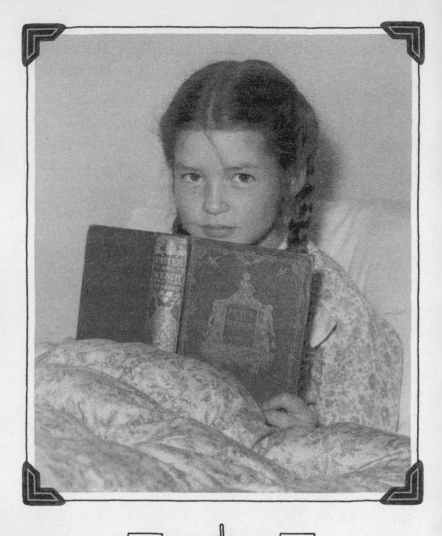

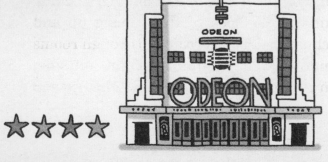

16
Mandy

I was taken to the cinema regularly. I didn't go to the children's Saturday morning pictures – Biddy thought that was too rowdy. I watched proper adult films, though the very first time I went I disgraced myself. This was at the Odeon in Surbiton, when I was three and still living at Fassett Road. All five of us – Biddy, Harry, Ga, Gongon and me – went to see some slapstick comedy. I didn't do a lot of laughing.

I thought it was all really happening before my very eyes (remember, we didn't have television in those days). I found it very worrying that these silly men were sometimes so big that their whole heads filled the screen. I couldn't work out where the rest of their bodies were. I knew I didn't want these giants coming anywhere near me. Then they shrank back small again. They were running away, pursued by even scarier men with hatchets. They dodged in and out of traffic in a demented fashion, then ran into a tall block of flats, going up and down lifts, charging along corridors, through rooms to the windows. They climbed right outside, wobbling on the edge. The camera switched so you saw things from their point of view, looking down down down, the cars below like little ants. The audience *laughed*. I screamed.

I had to be carted out of the cinema by Biddy and Harry, still screaming. They were cross because they'd wasted two one-and-ninepenny tickets.

'Why did you have to make such a fuss?' said Biddy.

'The man was going to fall!' I wailed.

'It wasn't *real*,' said Harry.

It took me a while to grasp this, which was odd seeing as I lived in my own imaginary world so much. However, I grew to love going to the cinema, though I never liked slapstick comedy, and I still hate it whenever there's a mad chase in any film.

We saw *Genevieve* together, and all three of us found that very funny indeed. Biddy said she thought Kay Kendall was beautiful. I thought this strange, because Kay Kendall had short dark hair. I didn't think you could possibly be beautiful unless you had blonde fairy-princess hair way past your shoulders.

Harry quite liked musicals but Biddy couldn't stand anything with singing, so Harry and I went to see *Carousel* and *South Pacific* together. I thought both films wondrously tragic. I don't think I understood a lot of the story but I loved all the romantic parts and all the special songs.

154

When Harry was in a very good mood, he'd sing as he got dressed in the morning – silly songs like 'Mairzie Doats an Doazie Doats' and 'She Wears Red Feathers and a Hooly-Hooly Skirt', and occasionally a rude Colonel Bogey song about Hitler. But now he'd la-la-la the *Carousel* roundabout theme tune while whirling around himself, or he'd prance about in his vest and pants singing, *'I'm going to wash that man right out of my hair.'*

I can't remember who took me to see *Mandy*. It was such an intense experience that the cinema could have crumbled around me and I wouldn't have noticed. I was *in* that film, suffering alongside Mandy. She was a little deaf girl who was sent away to a special boarding school to try to learn how to speak. There was a big sub-plot about her quarrelling parents and the developing relationship between Mandy's mother and the head teacher of the school, but that didn't interest me. I just watched Mandy, this small sad little girl with big soulful eyes and dark wispy plaits. I cried when she cried. When she mouthed 'Man-dee' at the end of the film, I whispered it with her.

I wanted to be Mandy's friend in the film and make her plasticine necklaces and play ball with her and comfort her when she couldn't sleep at night. I was old enough now to understand that the film wasn't real. Mandy was played by a child actress, Mandy Miller. I thought she was wonderfully gifted. Biddy showed me a photo in the *Sunday Mirror* of the real Mandy at the premiere of her film, and I realized she was much more glamorous in real life. She still had the spindly plaits, but instead of the pleated skirt and tartan windcheater she wore in the film, she was wearing a sophisticated silk party frock with puffed sleeves and a broderie anglaise collar and velvet ribbon at the neck and waist. She was even wearing *white gloves*.

I had a third Mandy in my head from then on, not the deaf child in the film, not the real actress. I had *my* Mandy, an imaginary friend with big eyes and dark plaits, and we were inseparable for years.

Biddy took me to see every Mandy Miller film that came out, though I wasn't allowed to see *Background* because it had an over-twelve rating, probably because it was about divorce. People thought so differently about divorce in those days. They frequently *whispered* the word. It was considered shameful, barely socially acceptable. It was the reason why so many incompatible couples stayed together. They didn't want to go through the public disgrace of a divorce. I thought this odd even then. In fact I used to pray my own parents *would* divorce because there were so many screaming fights now. Sometimes I was caught up in a quarrel too, both of them yelling at me, appealing to me, while I begged not to have to take sides. Sometimes I simply listened from my bedroom while they argued endlessly, whipping each other with cruel words, then slapping and shoving, hurting and hating.

Perhaps this was another reason why Mandy's films meant so much to me. She was in one or two child-centred fun films like *Raising a Riot* (about a family living in a windmill), but most of Mandy's films were about unhappy, anxious children living tense lives. My favourite Mandy film was *Dance Little Lady*, a colourful melodrama about a beautiful ballet dancer, her unscrupulous impresario husband and their only daughter, played by Mandy. The ballet dancer has a fall and can't work, the impresario loses interest in her, they fight bitterly – but they both love their little girl, a budding ballet dancer herself. Mandy does a proper dance in the film, her hair tied back with a satin ribbon, wearing an amazing cream, pink and turquoise beribboned tutu with white fishnet tights and pink ballet shoes.

There were no videos or DVDs in those days, of course, but I rewound that dance scene again and again inside my head. The film had a very dramatic ending. The father is in charge of Mandy one weekend but leaves her alone in their lodging house. There's a fire, Mandy is in peril, but the father comes rushing back and rescues her. She clings to him in her white nightie on the rooftop, the flames licking nearer and nearer. He manages to throw her to safety before he's engulfed by the flames himself. I thought it the most thrilling film ever, though I think I'd have severe reservations about it if I ever saw it again!

It might seem odd that I remember Mandy's films so vividly when I only saw most of them once – but I had a fantastic *aide-mémoire*. I kept my own scrapbook of any Mandy Miller photos I saw in newspapers or magazines, but these were just tiny blurred images. I also had a little attaché case bursting with big glossy Mandy photos, some of them 'stills' from her films, some specially taken publicity photos. Biddy looked at the photo copyright names in the papers, found out the right addresses and took me up to London with her to the film companies and press offices.

I was still a very shy child. I'd be paralysed with embarrassment when Biddy blagged her way through reception and then begged for Mandy Miller photos.

'It's for the kiddie, you see,' she'd say, nodding at me. 'She's mad about Mandy.'

I'd hang my head and blush scarlet, but nine times out of ten they'd soften and let us have several photos. Sometimes Biddy had to pay, but mostly we got them for nothing. Biddy would wrap them in tissue paper and carry them carefully on the tube and train in her shopping bag. When we got home, I could spread out my new photos and relive each film, frequently inventing new scenes, completely different new plots and characters to suit myself.

I used the film photos for most of my imaginary scenarios because Mandy looked sad or anxious or tragic and that gave me more scope. I felt more in touch with that Mandy. The Mandy photographed in her own home was a different girl entirely, a blessed child leading an idyllic life. I treasured a series of photos taken at her birthday party. Mandy's wearing a beautiful smocked Liberty frock, lighting the candles on her cake while her mother and her big sister and her friends smile at her.

Biddy didn't make birthday cakes. She *did* make lovely fairy cakes with lemon-flavoured icing and a walnut stuck on top. I liked them very much but they weren't quite the same as real birthday cake with icing and butter cream and special candles. I didn't have birthday parties either. Biddy said the flat was too small and she didn't have time to prepare for them as she went out to work. I was partly relieved because I'd have been horribly shy and scared that we wouldn't pass muster as a normal happy family, but I still felt a pang whenever I looked at the photo of Mandy's party.

At about the same time – she's wearing the same checked hair ribbons – there's a set of photos taken in her back garden. Mandy's playing in her tent and climbing a tree with a friend, and then she's swinging dangerously upside down from a branch, her plaits flying.

I didn't have my own garden – but I could play out in The Jungle, the huge overgrown wilderness behind the flats. I was very much a girl for playing *in*, but sometimes I went down to The Jungle with Sue, the little girl next door. We were both meek girls whose mothers fancied themselves a cut above the other residents. We were sent out to play in clean checked summer frocks, little white socks and polished sandals. We had enough sense to steer well away from the tough gangs, who would pull our hair, tug our skirts up to mock our white knickers and then push us into the nettles.

They had a rope attached to one of the tallest trees so you could swing like Tarzan. We swung too, timidly, and we both climbed the fir tree with the easiest branches, all the way to the top. One slip and we'd have broken our necks. It was just as well our mums never found out what we were up to.

Mandy had a white poodle, and there was a lovely photo of her giving him a big hug. I decided poodles were my favourite dogs too. I had a little black china poodle on my windowsill at home, and a kind old lady at Waverley Hall won a white furry poodle at bingo on Clacton Pier and gave it to me. I was overwhelmed, though this poodle quickly developed alopecia. His fur fell out, leaving ugly yellow glue stains, and then one of his glass eyes loosened and dangled out of his head, so Biddy put him in the dustbin.

When I got my Vip, I decided I loved Pekes most of all, but I've changed my mind now. I can't wait to have my little black miniature poodle.

Much to my joy, Mandy seemed a bookish girl. She was photographed several times with books spread all around her. My all-time favourite photograph of her shows her sitting up in bed in her flowery nightie, holding a gilt-embellished copy of *Peter and Wendy* by J. M. Barrie. I hope she's somehow hung onto that book. I've got a first edition of it myself, bought in my twenties for ten shillings – that's 50p in today's money. A first edition in a dust wrapper was recently auctioned for £3000!

I didn't know anything about the value of books as a child, but I did know the price of every doll, and I was seriously impressed that Mandy was photographed holding an Elizabeth doll. This was a special doll brought out to commemorate the Queen's Coronation in 1953. She wasn't a grown-up doll with a crown; she was a child doll with blonde curls and a cotton frock with a tight white plastic belt to match her neat white plastic shoes.

I longed for an Elizabeth doll but they were nearly three pounds – much too expensive. Biddy took me to see several shelves of them in Hamleys and they all smiled down at me, fanning their fingers in regal waves.

Which of my characters gets taken to Hamleys toyshop and longs to be given a special doll?

It's Dolphin in *The Illustrated Mum*.

We went to Hamleys in Oxford Street afterwards, a
special huge toy shop. Micky took us to look at the
dolls though even he could see that Star was past that
stage. I knew I should be too old for dolls too but I
ached with longing as I looked at all the specially
designed dolls locked away in glass cases. They had
beautiful gentle faces and long long long hair. My
fingers itched to comb it. They had wonderful romantic
outfits too, hand-sewn smocked dresses and ruched
pinafores and perfect little leather boots.

I leaned my forehead on the cold glass and stared
at them all, making up names for each one and
inventing their personalities. They all reached out for
me with their long white fingers. They looked so real
I was sure they couldn't be cold and stiff to touch. I

chose the one I liked the very best. She had long blonde curls and blue eyes and a dress and pinafore outfit the pink and blue of hyacinths, with pink silky socks and blue shoes fastened with little pearl buttons. I called her Natasha and knew she and I could be best friends for ever . . .

Children often ask me which is my favourite out of all my books. I tend to chop and change a little but I frequently choose *The Illustrated Mum*. I never re-read my books once they're published – I'd find it awkward and embarrassing and want to change things – but I've watched the beautiful television film of *The Illustrated Mum* several times, and I always end up in tears.

1953 CORONATION 1953

17

The Coronation

The Queen's Coronation was an enormous big deal in the 1950s. We thought differently about royalty then. They were like mysterious powerful gods with gold crowns permanently perched on their heads. Each school had a poster of the royal family in the hall entrance. The national anthem was frequently thumped out on the school piano while we all stood up straight, and woe betide you if you messed around or got the giggles. If you so much as sneezed during *'happy and glorious'*, you could get the cane. They didn't just play 'God Save the Queen' in schools. It was played at almost every public event, even at every cinema show down the Regal or the Odeon.

The country was in a state of feverish excitement before the Coronation. People plotted for weeks to work out how they could camp overnight on the route and catch a glimpse of Elizabeth in her gold carriage. There were little replicas of this gold carriage everywhere, complete with weeny horses. I hinted and hinted but didn't get lucky. My only Coronation memorabilia were the silver spoon and the blue china commemorative mug given free to every school child – and Harry broke my mug a week later. I expect the spoon might still be rattling about at the back of my mother's cutlery drawer somewhere. Maybe I'll try to reclaim it.

We didn't go up to London to see the Coronation. Biddy and Harry didn't see the point so I didn't get to wave my little Union Jack flag. However, we did *see* the Queen getting crowned. We got our first television so we could watch, along with hundreds of thousands of families all over the country. It was the talking point everywhere – who was forking out for an eleven-inch Bush television to see the Coronation. It was the first huge national event that the population could see simultaneously. We didn't have to rush to the cinema the next week and watch Pathé News. We could peep right inside Westminster Abbey and see the Archbishop of Canterbury place the crown on Elizabeth's head from the comfort of our own utility armchairs.

Biddy invited Ga and Gongon. The five of us watched the Coronation, with commentary by Richard Dimbleby – brother of the lady who declared I was an ultra-clean well-kept baby. We felt he was practically our best friend. We listened to his hushed, reverent tones, describing the scene we could see for ourselves in blurred black and white miniature.

We all knew it was a momentous occasion. It was also very very very boring. After half an hour of squatting on my little leatherette pouffe I sloped off to play with my paper dolls. I was reminded that this was a once-in-a-lifetime event and I should pay attention, but Biddy's telling-off was half-hearted. She was yawning and fidgeting herself. We weren't especially royalist in my family, though we'd read Crawfie's account of her life as a governess to little Lilibet and Margaret Rose, serialized in some women's magazine. Even so, Biddy bought a tea caddy with a picture of the newly crowned Queen looking very glamorous, and when full-colour souvenir books of the Coronation appeared in Woolworths, Biddy bought one. I leafed through the pages listlessly, but I liked the new Queen's crown and sceptre and orb – I was always a girl for flashy jewels.

We also went together to see a children's film called *John and Julie* later that year, about a little girl who runs away to see the Queen's Coronation. I thought the girl playing Julie was quite sweet, but not a patch on my Mandy.

Biddy kept the newspapers with the coverage of the Coronation in case they might be valuable one day. Maybe she's still got them. I wish she'd kept all my *Girl* comics instead!

There's certainly no mention of the Queen's Coronation in any of my books! I don't think there's anything about the royal family either. So OK, who lives in the Royal Hotel?

It's Elsa in *The Bed and Breakfast Star*.

We went to stay at the Royal Hotel. The Royal sounds very grand, doesn't it? And when we got down one end of the street and got our first glimpse of the Royal right at the other end, I thought it looked very grand too. I started to get excited. I'd never stayed in a great big posh hotel before. Maybe we'd all have our own rooms with satellite telly and people would make our beds and serve us our breakfasts from silver trays. As if we were Royalty staying in the Royal.

Maybe if Elsa achieves her big ambition to be a comedian, she might *just* be asked to take part in a Royal Variety Performance in front of the Queen.

18

Papers and Comics

We were a family with a hefty newspaper bill. Biddy liked the *Daily Mail* and Harry had the *Telegraph* and the *Sporting Life* and the *Racing Post*. Harry's biggest hobby was horse racing. He went to race meetings occasionally, and every Saturday afternoon he crouched in his armchair, fists clenched, watching the racing on our new television. He'd shout excitedly if his horse looked as if it had a chance – 'Come on, come on!' – jigging up and down as if he was riding the horse himself.

I don't know how much he won or lost, he never told us. He didn't put flamboyantly large amounts of money on any horse. Later on, when we had a telephone, I heard him place each-way bets for a few shillings, but he was a steady punter, betting every day there was a race on.

He kept every racing paper and form book and studied them religiously, jotting down numbers and marking likely names. He squashed his suits and trousers up into a tiny corner of his wardrobe so that he could store all this information inside.

He also bought a London evening paper on his

way home from work. There were three to choose from in those days. Newspaper sellers used to shout, '*Star, News* and *Stan-daaaard!*' over and over again. Harry bought the *Star*, the paper with the strip cartoon 'Tuppenny and Squibbit'.

I had my own comics too. I started off with a twee little baby comic called *Chick's Own*, where the hard words were hy-phe-na-ted, but soon I progressed to the much more rufty-tufty *Beano*. I liked the Bash Street Kids because the humour was imaginative and anarchic, but I'd have liked it to be a bit more girly. I read *Schoolfriend* and occasionally *Girls' Crystal*, but they were plain black-and-white comics. The most magical comic of all was *Girl*, well worth fourpence-halfpenny out of my shilling pocket money.

It was delivered every week. I was so entranced by some of the serial stories that I could barely wait for the next episode. I didn't really care for dark-haired schoolgirl Wendy and her blonde friend Jinx on the front cover, but I was a particular fan of Belle of the Ballet inside the comic. I talked about her enthusiastically to my teacher Mrs Symons and she gently corrected my pronunciation. Up till that moment I'd been calling her Belly of the Ballette.

The best serial was on the back page. Every week there were inspiring stories about special women, written by the Reverend Chad Varah. Sometimes these heroines were well known, like Florence

Nightingale, the Lady with the Lamp. Sometimes they were long-ago historical figures like Princess Adelaide, a particular favourite. Sometimes they were religious, like Mary Slessor, the mill girl from Dundee who became a missionary. Sometimes they ticked every single box, like Joan of Arc. I'd seen her picture in my nursery history book but I had no idea what happened to her. The last Joan of Arc picture strip was such a shock. The illustration of Joan standing in yellow flames, clutching her wooden cross, her eyes raised piously, made me shake with a complicated mixture of excitement, horror and pity.

I started to be stirred by current sad stories in the newspapers too. On Sundays Biddy liked to take the *Mirror* and the *News of the World* so she could have a good juicy read over her fried breakfast in bed. One summer they serialized Ruth Ellis's story while she was locked up in Holloway, the women's prison. I read over Biddy's shoulder. She tutted over Ruth's blonde hair and pencilled eyebrows and dark lips. 'She's obviously just a good-time girl. Look at that peroxide hair! Talk about common!'

I thought she looked glamorous and Ruth had always been one of my favourite names. I loved the story of Ruth and Naomi in Scripture at school, and there was another Ruth in a current favourite book, *The Tanglewood's Secret* by Patricia St John. It had made a big impression on me because a boy in that

175

book had climbed a tree, fallen and died. It had all been very sad, and Ruth and I had been very upset. This new true story about a real Ruth was about death too. She'd shot her boyfriend. I couldn't help sympathizing a little because it sounded as if he'd been horrible to her. But now she'd been tracked down and convicted of murder, and in a few weeks' time she was going to be hanged.

I hadn't really taken on board what capital punishment meant until then. It seemed a crazy idea. If society was so shocked that Ruth Ellis had killed someone, why was it right that *she* should be killed too, and in such an obscene and ritualistic way? I couldn't believe that anyone could legally drag a healthy person from their cell, put a noose around their neck and then hang them.

I didn't think they would ever go through with it. I thought it was just a threat to frighten her. I thought she'd get a last-minute reprieve.

She didn't. They went ahead with the whole grisly procedure. They hanged her at nine o'clock in the morning.

One of my books has wonderful illustrations set out at the beginning of each chapter, lots of little pictures in a strip, like the most imaginative and beautiful drawn comic. Which is it?

It's *Candyfloss*.

I'm so very lucky having Nick Sharratt illustrate my books. I think they're all brilliant illustrations but maybe *Candyfloss* is my favourite. We had fun with the very last page, putting in lots of familiar faces. See how many of the children you recognize!

19

Health

I started to brood about death after reading about Ruth Ellis. I hadn't really had anyone close to me die. Harry's mother had died when I was a baby. His father had died a few years later, but I hardly knew him. Maybe Ga and Gongon were next on the Grim Reaper's list. They weren't a robust couple. Gongon had a heart attack one Christmas when I was a child. He wasn't rushed to hospital. He stayed upstairs in bed and everyone tiptoed round, whispering and looking worried.

He made a full recovery but he was treated like an invalid after that. He retired early from work and sat in his armchair and sucked sadly on his pipe like an ancient old man when he must only have been in his fifties.

My grandmother wasn't in much of a position to wait on him hand and foot. Ga suffered from cripplingly painful arthritis. She changes quickly in the family photo album from a little blonde woman with a curvy figure to a fat old lady in longish skirts and granny shoes. Maybe her steroid treatments made her put on weight. She ate exactly the same as my grandfather and yet he was matchstick-thin.

Once a month she went up to a London hospital and tried every treatment going. She even had gold injections for a while. I hoped her teeth and fingernails might suddenly gleam gold, but there was no external evidence of this treatment whatsoever and I don't think it helped much internally either. She was in constant severe pain. Sometimes she could hardly get out of her armchair, and her face would screw up in agony, but she never once cried.

Her poor hands were so badly affected that her fingers became claws and she couldn't sew any more. Many years later, when I had my daughter Emma, Ga struggled desperately, her lips clamped together, and knitted her little dresses and cardigans and tiny woollen buttoned shoes, and crocheted an enormous soft white shawl. *I* want to cry when I think of all that painful effort.

She had a new hip put in and there was talk of new knees, but there was a limit to what they could do. Her feet swelled with bunions and in her later years she could barely walk.

But neither grandparent died when I was young. Biddy and Harry stayed reasonably healthy too. Biddy had frequent heavy colds like me. (I had *just* as many colds after my tonsils had been pulled out.)

They always went to her chest and made her cough, but this was probably because she smoked so much. Her chic red packets of Du Maurier cigarettes were part of her, like her Max Factor Crème Puff powder and her Coty L'Aimant perfume. She smoked like a chimney, she sucked clove sweets and pear drops and humbugs, she ate Mars bars constantly, childishly chewing along the top, saving the toffee part till last. She wouldn't walk for more than two minutes in her high heels and determinedly took no exercise whatsoever – and yet she's still going strong now, in her mid-eighties.

Harry never smoked and didn't have a sweet tooth. He had odd tastes in food. He'd eat peanuts from the shell, cracking them into newspaper in the evenings as he watched television. He'd construct his own odd little teas of beetroot and St Ivel cheese. He rarely cooked, but he had his own particular specialities, like very good tinned-salmon fishcakes. He ate healthily, if weirdly, and he took masses of exercise, cycling all the way up to London and back every day. He frequently went for long walks and he was also a very active member of the local tennis club. He seemed fit as a fiddle – but his heart started playing up and he died when he was only fifty-seven.

Maybe it was because of all his temper tantrums. When he was in full rant, his face would go an ugly red and the veins would stand out on his forehead. We could never tell when one of these terrifying temper fits would start up. Sometimes they came out of nowhere. Other times Biddy seemed to go out of her way to provoke him.

'He's got a terrible inferiority complex, that's why he gets into these states,' she said.

She didn't see why she should try to make a fuss of him and boost his confidence.

'I'm not going to *pretend*,' she said, outraged at the idea. 'It's not my way. If I think he's useless, I'll say so.'

She did, repeatedly. When she got a job as a book-keeper at Prince Machines and they had a firm's dance, she insisted that Harry go with her. Surprisingly, he agreed, but the evening wasn't a success.

'He just sat there like a lemon, wouldn't say a word,' Biddy raged. 'He wouldn't even dance with anyone, not even when this woman begged him. I was so embarrassed!'

'For God's sake, she was *drunk*,' said Harry. 'And it wasn't a dance – she wanted me to join in these damn daft party games.'

Biddy had started playing her own private game with a man called Ron who worked at Prince Machines. Surely that was part of the reason for all the rows? Yet they never seemed to argue about him. Ron was almost like part of our family – *Uncle* Ron to me. When I was old enough to be left on Saturday evenings, Biddy *and* Harry went out with Uncle Ron. They mostly went to pubs, which was the strangest thing of all, because they were both still teetotal. Maybe they sipped bitter lemons all evening.

We even had a joint holiday together, with Uncle Ron's wife Grace, who understandably didn't seem keen on this weird situation.

I plucked up courage recently to ask Biddy if Harry realized what was going on under his nose.

'I don't know,' she said impatiently. 'We didn't ever discuss it.'

I always knew about Uncle Ron – and several other uncles – and I certainly wasn't going to blab to my dad, but I did think it horribly unfair to him. I didn't *like* my dad and he could be incredibly alarming and unkind, but I always felt sorry for him. It wasn't until he got ill that I realized there were not one but two 'aunties' lurking in the background, both of whom came to his funeral.

They both told me – separately – how much my dad had loved me and been proud of me. I was astonished. I couldn't remember him saying anything of the sort to me. In fact several times he'd told me he couldn't stand me.

Perhaps they were just being kind and felt it was the polite thing to say at funerals.

Yet sometimes he acted like he really *did* love me, even if he never said so. That's what's so puzzling about writing a true story. If I was making my story up, I'd invent a consistent father, good or bad. Real people change so. Harry might have been a bad father to me in many ways, but he lived long enough to be a wonderful caring grandfather to Emma, patiently playing with her for hours, never once losing his temper.

Harry could sometimes be gentle and imaginative with me too. He had a passion for the countryside and as soon as we moved to Cumberland House he'd pore over maps and go for bike rides round the Surrey lanes. When I was on holiday from school, he'd take a day off from work and take me for a long country outing. We'd walk the Pilgrim's Way, stand beside the deep green Silent Pool and struggle up the slippery chalk paths of Box Hill. We'd pick blackberries or hazelnuts, or buy bags of tomatoes to supplement our cheese sandwich picnics.

I was a weedy little girl but I could walk seven or eight miles in my sturdy Clarks sandals. Harry was generally at his best on these occasions. He'd let me chatter and he'd sometimes join in my imaginary games in a desultory fashion. We watched an adaptation of Robert Louis Stevenson's *Kidnapped* on the television and played we were Davie and Alan wandering through the woods. Well, I played, and Harry trudged along, nodding every now and then. Sometimes he'd tell me the name of his favourite racehorse and I'd gallop along beside him, pretending to be winning my race.

We sometimes took the train to Guildford. Before setting out for the surrounding fields and hills Harry would take me to the big second-hand bookshop at the top of the town. It was a huge dark muddle of a shop with long corridors and sudden steps up and down and a series of connecting rooms, but if you negotiated this labyrinth properly, you found a whole room of children's books.

Harry had a happy knack of finding me a book I'd like. He was a member of the Westminster Public Library near his office at the Treasury, and he sometimes borrowed a book for me. He brought home *Marianne Dreams* by Catherine Storr, a magical book about two sick children who draw themselves into a nightmare world of their imagination. It had a profound effect on me. I was very careful not to draw anything too scary with my best Venus HB pencil after that, just in case.

He also brought me an adult book, *The River* by Rumer Godden, about a family of children in India. I was only eight or nine. I found it hard to get into the first few pages, but when I got used to Rumer's strange style, I *adored* it. I particularly identified with Harriet, the intense literary child-narrator. Biddy had considered calling me Harriet, as an amalgamation of Harry and her own real first name, Margaret. She'd decided against this idea because she thought Harriet such a plain old-fashioned name. I was a plain old-fashioned child and *longed* to be called Harriet. I didn't care for the name Jacqueline at all, especially the way Biddy said it when she was cross with me – *'Jacqueline!'* Still, the other name under consideration had apparently been Babette, so maybe I got off lightly.

Two sisters in one of my books have a grandma with very bad arthritis. Can you remember who they are?

They're Ruby and Garnet, the identical twins in *Double Act*.

> Gran's arthritis got worse. She'd always had funny fingers and a bad hip and a naughty knee. But soon she got so she'd screw up her face when she got up or sat down, and her fingers welled sideways and she couldn't make them work.

That's Garnet doing the talking. I found it an interesting challenge swapping from one twin to the other, so that they both get to write their story. Sometimes people don't realize that there are *two* illustrators for *Double Act*. Nick Sharratt does all the Ruby drawings, and Nick's friend Sue Heap does all the Garnet drawings. They have similar styles. It's fun flicking through the book quickly, deciding which picture was drawn by Nick and which by Sue.

20

Biddy

Biddy was very happy to go out to work. Harry only gave her a meagre amount for housekeeping and she hated being dependent on him. She worked at Roberts the cake shop first. I thoroughly enjoyed all the extra bath buns and currant slices and apple puffs.

Then she got a job as a playground lady in Kingsnympton Juniors, though this was the very school she'd turned down for me. Biddy was strict with me and expected me to know my place and to say please and thank-you. I must never interrupt. I must never say 'What?' if I didn't hear her. I had to rattle through 'I'm sorry, what did you say?' I certainly mustn't say 'Pardon' because that was common. 'Toilet' was common too. We said 'lav' in our family, and we used genteel euphemisms for what we did *in* the lav. It must have been a terrible trial for Biddy to be surrounded by ordinary, lively, cheeky council estate kids. That job didn't last long.

She tried taking the newspapers round to all the patients in Kingston Hospital. This was a job she loved, especially going round the men's wards chatting them all up. She took me with her in the summer holidays. I wasn't allowed on the wards, but I'd wait outside in the hospital gardens. I'd have a book with me, and I'd take a handful of my favourite paper girls and sit swinging my legs on a bench, carefully fanning my girls out on my lap. Sometimes a nurse or a cleaner would come and have a little chat with me. One elderly lady was especially kind and gave me the odd sweet or two. Biddy had drummed it into me never to take sweets from strangers but I knew the old lady was just being friendly.

These were part-time jobs. Biddy branched out and got a full-time job at Prince Machines when I was eight. She stayed there the longest of all her jobs, probably because of Uncle Ron. Then she worked in an office up in London, behind the scenes in Bentalls department store, and then in the finance office of Kingston Polytechnic. She even worked as a cocktail barmaid for one evening but gave up because she didn't have a clue what any of the drinks were. Eventually she set herself up in a small way as an antique dealer. She traded in Richmond for years, and then kept a small stall in the local antique centre well into her eighties. Even now she bids over-enthusiastically on eBay.

In the days of my childhood she had no spare cash whatsoever, but she managed to be inventive with her money. We never ate out as a family but Biddy and I had secret treat lunches together. We went to Joe Lyons in Kingston after a Saturday shop. We always had tomato soup, fish and chips, and strawberry mousse. She also took me to Winifred's, a small café on Kingston Hill that specialized in home-cooked food: steak-and-kidney pies, or sausage and mash, or a roast and three veg. They had proper puddings too, like baked jam roll with custard, much appreciated by the elderly male clientele.

I remember reading a *Woman's Companion* one day while we were waiting to be served. I was only eight or nine, but it was one of my favourite journals, a lowbrow story magazine with a pale red cover. I particularly liked the problem page, though there were sometimes words I didn't understand.

'Mummy,' I piped up, 'what are periods?'

I knew by the embarrassed coughs and rustles all around me that I'd somehow spoken out of turn.

'I'll tell you later,' Biddy hissed – and fair enough, she did.

We had our jaunts up to London to look at the dolls and beg for Mandy photos. We also went to the big C & A clothes shop in Oxford Street to look at the party dresses. I hankered after the flouncy satin dresses – bright pinks and harsh blues and stinging yellows – but Biddy thought these *very* common. She chose for me a little white dress with delicate stripes

191

and multi-coloured smocking and a lace collar. I still preferred the tarty satin numbers, but I loved my demure pretty frock and called it my rainbow dress.

I *didn't* love the trying-on process. Biddy was always in a hurry, and if there was a long queue for the changing room, she pulled off my coat and tugged my dress over my head, leaving me utterly exposed in my vest and knickers. I protested bitterly, scarlet-faced.

'Don't be so silly,' said Biddy. 'Who on earth would want to look at *you*?'

She was forever putting me in my place and reminding me not to get above myself. If I got over-excited at a dance or a party and joined in noisily with all the other children, Biddy would seize hold of me and hiss in my ear, 'Stop showing off!' Yet this was the same mother who wanted me to turn into Shirley Temple and be the all-singing, all-dancing little trouper at a talent show.

She had no patience with my moans and groans but she could be a very concerned mother at times. When I was seven or eight, I developed a constant cough that wouldn't go away even when she'd spooned a whole bottle of Veno's down me. She was always worried about my chest since my bout of bronchitis so she carted me off to the doctor.

He didn't find anything seriously wrong with me. I think now it was probably a nervous cough, an anxious reaction to the tension at home. The doctor advised Sea Air as if I was a Victorian consumptive.

'Sea Air!' said Biddy.

We lived seventy miles from the seaside and we didn't have a car. But she took it on board valiantly. She somehow managed to find the money to take me on Saturday coach trips to Brighton right the way through the winter. We mooched round the antique shops in The Lanes and had a cup of tea and a bun in a café and walked up and down the pier and shivered in deckchairs while I breathed in the Sea Air. It worked a treat.

You certainly didn't go to Biddy for tea and sympathy, but she was brilliant at getting things done. She was almost too good when it came to school projects. I remember a nature project when we were told to collect examples of different leaves. This was a simple enough project. I could easily gather up a handful of leaves on my way home from school. But when I casually mentioned it to Biddy, she snapped into action. She dispatched Harry and me to Richmond Park on Sunday morning and instructed us to find at least twenty different samples. We did as we were told. Biddy spread leaves, berries, nuts – goodness knows what else – all over the living-room table. It was our job to identify each example with an inadequate I-Spy spotters' guide, *her* job to mount them magnificently on special white board. She labelled them in her exquisitely neat handwriting, then covered the finished work of art with protective cellophane.

My arms ached horribly carrying this confection like a splendid over-sized tray on the half-hour walk to school. The other children claimed – justifiably – that I'd cheated. The teacher seemed under-impressed with Biddy's showy display. I had enough sense to lie like crazy when I got back home, telling Biddy that I'd been highly praised and given top marks for my project.

She particularly excelled at Christmas presents. She had no truck with Father Christmas, not seeing why he should get the kudos when she'd done all the hard work and spent the money. I didn't feel at all deprived. I didn't care for Father Christmas either. I hated having to queue up to have my photo taken with this overly jolly old gent in Bentalls department store at Christmas. Once he'd peered myopically at my short-cropped hair and given me a blue-wrapped present for a boy.

We didn't go in for stockings at Cumberland House. Biddy organized a special Christmas bumper *box* stuffed with goodies wrapped in bright tissue paper. There might be a Puffin paperback – *Ballet Shoes* or *The Secret Garden* or *The Children Who Lived in a Barn*. There would definitely be a shiny sheath of Mandy photos. I'd hold them

194

carefully and very lightly trace her glossy plaits, smiling back at her. There could be crayons or a silver biro, and red and blue notebooks from Woolworths with the times tables and curious weights and measures printed on the back. I never encountered these rods, poles and pecks in my arithmetic lessons, and didn't want to either. There would be something 'nobby' – Biddy's favourite word of approval for a novelty item like an elephant pencil sharpener or two magnetic Scottie dogs that clung together crazily.

These were all extras. I always had a Main Present too. Hard-up though she was, Biddy never fobbed me off with clothes or necessities like a school satchel or a new eiderdown. My Main Present was a doll, right up until I got to double figures.

They were always very special dolls too. Sometimes I knew about them already. Once I saw a teenage rag doll with a daffodil-yellow ponytail and turquoise jeans in a shop window in Kingston and I ached to possess her. Biddy didn't think much of rag dolls but she could see just how much I wanted her. We'd go to look at her every week. I went on and on wanting her. Then one Saturday she wasn't there any more.

'Oh *dear*,' said Biddy, shaking her head – but she could never fool me.

I pretended to be distraught – and probably didn't fool her either. I waited until I was on my own in the flat, then hauled one of the living-room chairs into my parents' bedroom, opened Biddy's wardrobe door, and clambered up. There on the top shelf was a navy parcel, long but soft when I poked. It was the teenage rag doll, safely bought and hidden away.

I'd go and whisper to her at every opportunity, imagining her so fiercely she seemed to wriggle out of her wrapping paper, slide out from the pile of Biddy's scarves and hats, and climb all the way down her quilted dressing gown to play with me. My imagination embellished her a little too extravagantly. When I opened her up at long last on Christmas Day, her bland sewn face with dot eyes and a red crescent-moon smile seemed crude and ordinary. How could *she* be my amazing teenage friend?

Another Christmas I had a more sophisticated teenage doll, a very glamorous Italian doll with long brown hair and big brown eyes with fluttering eyelashes. She wore a stylish suedette jacket and little denim jeans and tiny strappy sandals with heels. When I undressed her, I was tremendously impressed to see she had real bosoms. This was a world before Barbie. She must have been one of the first properly modelled teenage dolls. I was totally in awe of her.

I had been reading in Biddy's *Sunday Mirror* about Princess Ira, a fifteen-year-old precociously beautiful Italian girl who was involved with a much older man. I called my doll Ira and she flaunted herself all round my bedroom, posing and wiggling and chatting up imaginary unsuitable boyfriends. I shuffled after her, changing her outfits like a devoted handmaid.

I had one real china doll from Biddy. She saved up ten shillings (fifty pence, but a fortune to us in those days) and bought her from an antique shop in Kingston. She wasn't quite a Mabel. She had limp mousy hair and had clearly knocked around a little. She was missing a few fingers and she had a chip on her nose but she still had a very sweet expression. I loved her, and her Victorian clothes fascinated me – all those layers of petticoats and then frilly drawers, but she was difficult to *play* with. She was large and unwieldy and yet terrifyingly fragile. I could move her arms and legs but they creaked ominously. I brushed her real hair but it came out in alarming handfuls, and soon I could see her white cloth scalp through her thinning hair.

I *wish* Biddy had been fiercer with me and made me keep her in pristine condition. She'd be happy living in my Victorian house. I'd never let some silly little girl undress her down to her drawers and comb her soft hair. She never really came alive for me. I can't even remember her name.

The best Christmas dolls ever were my Old Cottage twins. Old Cottage dolls were very special. I'd mist up the special glass display case peeping at them in Hamleys. They were quite small but wondrously detailed: hand-made little dolls with soft felt skin, somehow wired inside so they could stand and stride and sit down. One Old Cottage doll in little jodhpurs and black leather boots could even leap up on her toy horse and gallop. The dolls were dressed in a variety of costumes. You could choose an old-fashioned crinoline doll, an Easter bonnet girl, even a fairy in a silver dress and wings. I preferred the Old Cottage girls in ordinary everyday clothes – gingham dresses with little white socks and felt shoes. Every doll had a slightly different face and they all had different hairstyles. Some were dark, some were fair; some had curls, but most had little plaits, carefully tied.

Biddy knew which I'd like best. She chose a blonde girl with plaits and a dark girl with plaits, one in a blue flowery dress, one in red checks. Then she handed them over to Ga. She must have been stitching in secret for weeks and weeks. When I opened my box on Christmas morning, it was a wondrous treasure chest. I unwrapped my Old

Cottage twins and fell passionately in love with them at first sight. Then I opened a large wicker basket and discovered their *clothes*. Ga had made them little camel winter coats trimmed with fur, pink party dresses, soft little white nighties and tiny tartan dressing gowns, and a school uniform each – a navy blazer with an embroidered badge, a white shirt with a proper little tie, a pleated tunic, even two small felt school satchels.

I was in a daze of delight all Christmas Day. I could hardly bear to put my girls down so that I could eat up my turkey and Christmas pudding. I'd give anything to have those little dolls now with their lovingly stitched extensive wardrobe.

There's a Christmas scene at the start and end of one of my books. Which do you think it is?

It's *Clean Break*.

I was getting too big to believe in Santa but he still wanted to please me. I found a little orange journal with its own key; a tiny red heart soap; a purple gel pen; cherry bobbles for my hair; a tiny tin of violet sweets; a Jenna Williams bookmark; and a small pot of silver glitter nail varnish.

But Em thinks it's going to be the best Christmas ever, especially when her stepdad gives her a real emerald ring – but it all goes horribly wrong. She has a tough time throughout the next year, but it's Christmas Eve again in the last chapter. Someone comes knocking at the door and it looks as if this really *will* be a wonderful Christmas.

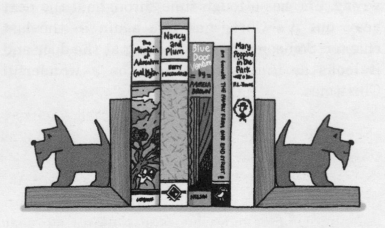

21

Books

Whenever I read writers' autobiographies, I always love that early chapter when they write about their favourite children's books. I was a total book-a-day girl, the most frequent borrower from Kingston Public Library. I think I spent half my childhood in the library. It meant so much to me to borrow books every week. It gives me such joy now to know that *I*'m currently the most borrowed author in British libraries.

In those other autobiographies people mention maybe six favourites, or select their top ten fiction characters. I can't choose! I feel as if I'm juggling my way through thousands of books, standing in a stadium jam-packed with fiction characters. They're all waving at me and mouthing, *Pick me! Pick me!*

I'll pick Enid Blyton first. She wasn't ever my favourite author but she got me *reading*. I pored over Pookie the white rabbit and the Shelf Animal books, but I couldn't work out what each word said. Then I went to school in Lewisham and learned that the c-a-t sat on the m-a-t, but I didn't really call that reading because it was so slow and laborious and there wasn't a real story.

I can't remember the magic moment when it all came together and I stopped stabbing the words with my finger and muttering each sound. I could suddenly just *do* it. Harry had read me all three Faraway Tree books and now I read them too. I spent months and months reading all the Enid Blytons I could find in the library. I didn't have to think about it. I didn't have to struggle with a single word. I didn't have to strain to understand what was going on. I could just let my eyes glide over the comfortably big print and experience all her different worlds.

Unlike most children, I didn't care for the Blyton mystery stories. I found the Secret Sevens and the Famous Fives boring. None of the children seemed to have much personality apart from George. I always like to read about fierce tomboy girls, though I was mostly a meek girly-girl myself.

I *did* rather enjoy some of the Adventure books. I owned a second-hand copy of *The Mountain of Adventure*. Somewhere in this book – presumably up the mountain – the children discovered a cave behind a waterfall and set up some sort of camp there. It seemed an incredibly romantic concept to me. I'd crawl under the living-room table with a doll or two and pretend the checked tablecloth was the waterfall. There was another underground cave in the book, filled with medieval religious figurines studded with jewels. I found this an awe-inspiring chapter too. We weren't a religious family and I'd certainly never been in a Catholic church, but somehow I'd seen a statue of a Madonna holding baby Jesus. I thought she was beautiful. The idea of a whole heavenly host of Madonnas cradling a nursery of Holy Infants was captivating. I imagined them taller than me, with real sapphires for eyes and solid gold haloes on their heads like celestial hats.

Even so, I preferred Blyton in more everyday mode. She wrote a book I particularly liked called *Hollow Tree House* about two children who run away and hide in – where else? – a hollow tree. I longed passionately for my own tree house, and planned, down to the finest detail, the things I would keep there (my favourite books, my Woolworths notebooks, my drawing book and tin of crayons, my Mandy photos), as if I thought I could conjure a sturdy tree growing out of our concrete balcony. There were plenty in the wilderness behind the flats, but I had no way of claiming personal ownership and no one to build me my house. Still, I was good at imaginary tree houses. Ann and I shared one in the playground at Latchmere, so it was not too difficult to pretend one for my own personal use at home.

I liked Enid Blyton's St Clare's school stories too. I had no desire whatsoever to go to boarding school myself. I was appalled at the idea of being in the company of other children all the time, with no opportunities whatsoever for private imaginary games, but it was fun to read about such a strangely different environment. The twins themselves were a little dull, but I liked Carlotta, the dashing circus girl, and Claudine, the naughty French girl – both apparently based on *real* girls.

I knew this because I'd solemnly read Enid Blyton's *The Story of My Life*. Some of the chapters were a bit of a struggle because I was still only about six or seven, but I found some passages riveting. I was interested to learn that little girl Enid had nightmares too, and she gave sensible practical tips on how to cope with them. She wrote about her own imaginary worlds. It was such a relief to realize that someone else had a weird vivid inner life like my own. It was fascinating learning about her writing routine. In those days children didn't know very much about their favourite authors. Sometimes they had baffling names like Richmal Crompton or P. L. Travers so you didn't even know whether they were men or women.

So Enid Blyton got me reading fluently and reinforced my desire to write, though I knew right from a very early age that I wanted to write very different sort of books. I wanted to write books that didn't seem to exist yet – books about realistic children who had difficult parents and all sorts of secrets and problems; easy-to-read books that still made you think hard; books with funny bits that made you laugh out loud, though sometimes the story was so sad it made you cry too.

I took to reading adult books *about* children, like Catherine Cookson's series about a tough little Tyneside girl called Mary Ann. She came from a very poor family and her beloved dad was a drunk, forever letting them down. Mary Ann was a devout Catholic and popped into the church the way other kids bobbed into the chip shop. She had Mary, Joseph and Jesus as her own personal ultra-good imaginary friends.

I envied Mary Ann and wished I was a Catholic too, especially if it meant saying prayers to beautiful statues of Mary. I'm not a Catholic, I'm still not at all religious, but gentle Madonnas – plaster, china, glass and wood – grace many corners of my house.

The only book written for children that struck me in any way as realistic was *The Family from One End Street* by Eve Garnett. It's a story about a poor family. Dad's a dustman, Mum's a washerwoman, and there are seven children. I wasn't so interested in reading about the boys but I loved the two oldest sisters, Lily Rose and Kate. Lily Rose was lumpy and helpful and took her responsibilities as a big sister seriously. She helped Mum with her ironing but had a terrible accident with the hot iron on a green artificial-silk petticoat. Kate was thin and clever and passed her exams to go to grammar school. She was so proud of her smart new uniform that she insisted on wearing it on a day trip to the seaside – a *big* mistake.

These girls seemed real to me, and they looked real too in Eve Garnett's drawings. They had straggly hair that stuck out at odd angles, their dresses had saggy hems and they wore plimsolls instead of shoes, just like most of the children I knew. Not me though. Biddy would have died if *I*'d looked like a child from a council estate. She had my hair viciously permed so that I looked as if I'd been plugged into an electric light socket.

She struggled to buy me new clothes every year. She wasn't having her daughter a Second-hand Rose with a telltale line around the coat hem where it had been let down. She *certainly* wasn't going to let me run around in plimsolls. I had Clarks strapover shoes in winter and brown sandals in the summer to wear to school, and strappy black patent shoes and snow-white sandals for best. No child was better shod. If my shoe heels ever got worn down, Harry would squat in the kitchen with a little cobbler's last and tap in 'Blakies' to make them last longer.

My favourite children's book at that time – well, maybe first equal with *Adventures with Rosalind*, was *Nancy and Plum* by Betty MacDonald. I read it so many times I knew long passages by heart. I suffered with them at Mrs Monday's orphanage, hurried anxiously beside them when they ran away, and celebrated when they met up with the kindly Campbells. They adopted Nancy and Plum and gave them lots of hugs and cuddles and chicken pies and beautiful dolls and lovely girly outfits.

I knew perfectly well this wasn't *likely* but I didn't care. I thought *Nancy and Plum* a perfect book. I also enjoyed a story by Betty MacDonald's sister called *Best Friends* – now there's a familiar title. In *this Best Friends* Suzie makes friends with Coco next door and they have fun together and share a tree house. Children's books in the 1950s sprouted veritable forests of tree houses.

I didn't only like books about poor or under-privileged children. I loved all the Mary Poppins books about the solidly middle-class Banks children, with their cook and their boot boy – and of course their magical nanny, Mary Poppins. I borrowed most of the Mary Poppins books from the library, reading them in reverse order and waiting weeks and weeks before I found the first in the series back on the shelf.

I begged Biddy to let me belong to a book club because *Mary Poppins in the Park* was the introductory book, available for just a few shillings. She gave in, so I got my very own yellow Mary Poppins book. I took it to school and carried it around with me all day. I then received a book club book a month, none of which were so much to my taste – Kitty Barnes, Malcolm Saville, Lorna Hill – all very worthy popular authors but they just didn't do it for me. However, there was one Pamela Brown book among the book club choices and I'd soon read my way along all the Browns on the shelf in the library. I particularly liked her Blue Door series about a group of children who set up their own theatre.

Pamela Brown wrote the first in the series when she was only fifteen, a fact that impressed me greatly. I wondered if any of my stories in my Woolworths exercise books would ever get published. They were mostly family stories about misunderstood children (surprise!), but I also wrote about girls who could fly, sad Victorian tales about poor little beggar children, comical fantasy stories, melodramatic love stories, even a very long retelling of the story of Moses from his sister Miriam's point of view. I didn't *really* believe I had a chance of seeing my stories in print. It was a daydream, like some little girls long to be actresses or rock stars or fashion models.

In one of my books I pretend there's going to be a special children's television serial based on Enid Blyton's book The Twins at St Clare's. *Who is desperate to get a part in it?*

It's Ruby in *Double Act*. But her twin, poor Garnet,
is appalled at the idea.

I can't act.

I don't *want* to act.

I can't go to an audition in London!
I can't say a lot of stuff with everyone
watching. It'll be even worse than
being a sheep. Why won't Ruby
understand? She won't listen to me.
She's riffling through *The Twins at St
Clare's* right this minute, trying to
choose which bit we'll act out.

Only I'm not going to act.

I can't can't can't act.

I can't act either, but I had a tiny part in the
television serial of *Double Act*. When Yvonne, the
producer, asked me if I wanted to take part myself,
I thought it would be fun. I thought I knew the
perfect part for me. Ruby and Garnet's dad has his
own second-hand bookshop. I am famous for my
vast collection of books (around 15,000! There are
shelves all over my house *and* a special little library
at the bottom of my garden). I won't be able to
read all my books even if I live to be 500, but I still
can't stop buying them. So I thought it would be
fun if I played a customer in the Red Bookshop. I

thought it might make children chuckle if they spotted me in a dark corner of the bookshop, happily browsing.

Yvonne had other ideas. She wanted me to play the fictional casting director who puts the twins through their paces at the audition. As she's been drawn in the book with short hair, flamboyant jewellery and extraordinary boots, I suppose it's easy to guess why Yvonne saw me in the part. But this meant I had to learn lines. I found this extraordinarily difficult. I just couldn't remember them – even though I *wrote* the lines myself!

I managed to stagger through somehow, but decided I'd definitely stick to my day job – writing – in future!

22

The Boys and Girls Exhibition

I got to meet Pamela Brown when I was nine. They used to hold a special Boys and Girls Exhibition at Olympia and Biddy took me one Saturday. I found it a very overwhelming day. The sheer *noise* of thousands of over-excited children in a vast echoing building made my ears throb. We were pushed and pummelled as we struggled round all the stands. Biddy was a pushy woman too, and occasionally batted a child out of her way. There was a lot of argy-bargy, mostly between mothers desperate to get their own kids to the front of each queue.

I wished Biddy had left me languishing at the back of the most popular stand, George Cansdale and his animals. George Cansdale was an animal expert and had his own programme on children's television. I wasn't as passionately fond of animals as most children, apart from my constant yearning for a dog. I didn't like anything creepy-crawly at all, and kept well away from anything with beaks or sharp claws.

George Cansdale had a whole enclosure of animals with him. All the children at Olympia wanted to stroke the rabbits and guinea pigs and kittens. Biddy shoved me from the back until I was practically catapulted onto George Cansdale's lap. He nodded at me as he sank his hands deep into a strange big coffin-shaped box.

'Hello, little girl. What's your name?' he said, starting to haul something heavy from the box.

'Jacqueline, sir,' I said.

Oh, we were so polite in the fifties. I practically bobbed a curtsey.

'You seem a very sensible little girl, Jacqueline,' said George Cansdale. 'Shall we show the other children just how sensible you are?'

He was still hauling what looked like enormous skeins of khaki wool from the box. Loop after loop. Coil after coil. A snake! An enormous brown snake, with a mean head and a forked tongue flicking in and out.

There was a great gasp, a collective series of *Beano*-comic exclamations: *'Aah!' 'Ugh!' 'Eek!'*

I was so shocked I couldn't even scream. I couldn't back away because I had Biddy and hundreds of children pressing hard against me.

'You're not scared of snakes, are you, Jacqueline?' said George Cansdale.

I bared my teeth in a sickly grin.

'Shall we show the other children how sensible you are?' he said, reaching towards me, his arms full of writhing snake.

He wound it round and round and round my neck like a loathsome live scarf.

'There! Look how brave Jacqueline is,' said George Cansdale.

The children oohed and aahed at me. I stood still, the head of the snake an inch away, its tongue going flicker flicker flicker in my face.

'There! Nothing to be frightened of, is there, Jacqueline?' said George Cansdale.

I was way past *fright*. Any second now I was going to wet myself. Mercifully, George Cansdale unwound the snake coil by coil until I was free at last. Biddy gave me a tug and tunnelled us through the crowd to the ladies' toilets.

'Why did you let him put that horrible slimy snake round you?' Biddy said, dabbing anxiously at the velvet collar on my coat.

'It wasn't slimy, it was *warm*,' I said, shuddering. 'Oh, Mum, it felt *awful*.'

'Well, you should have said something, not stood there looking gormless,' said Biddy, but she gave me a quick hug nevertheless.

That should have been enough excitement for one day, but Biddy was determined to get her money's worth. We went to a kind of Mind Body

Spirit section and had our bumps read by a shy man in spectacles still wearing a shabby brown demob suit. I'm surprised Biddy went for this, because his nervous fingers probed deep into our perms as he felt for significant bumps on our heads, wrecking our hairdos. Perhaps she was at a crisis point with Uncle Ron and wanted to see what fate had in store for her.

The Bump Man seemed disconcerted by Biddy's head.

'You're a real Peter Pan,' he said.

This pleased her no end, because she thought this meant she looked young for her age – which she did. He fumbled about in her curls, pressing and prodding, as if her head was a musical instrument and might start playing a tune. He said she was very bright and very determined. Then he ran out of steam and decided to do a bit of handwriting interpretation instead, maybe to reassure her she was getting her money's worth.

Biddy smiled happily. She always took great pride in her beautiful handwriting. The rare times she wrote a letter she always drafted it first and then copied it all out exquisitely in pen. The Bump Man admired her handwriting and said she was exceptionally neat and meticulous, which wasn't really straining his psychic powers.

Then it was my turn. I wrote my own much

shakier signature. We were being mucked about at school. Every year the new teacher had different ideas about handwriting. I was currently in a class where we were all forced to write in very sloping copperplate with blotchy dipping pens and brown school ink. My natural handwriting was little and stood upright, so I was struggling. The Bump Man said my personality was still forming. He felt my head too, not so nervous of me, kneading it as if it was an awkward lump of dough. He asked me various silly questions and I muttered answers in monosyllables.

'She's very shy,' said the Bump Man. 'What do you like doing best, dear?'

'Reading,' I whispered.

'Mm. Yes. You're very dreamy.'

'You're telling me!' said Biddy. 'I sometimes think she's not all there. What do you think she'll be when she grows up?'

'Oh, a teacher, definitely,' he said.

I was bitterly disappointed. I so so so wanted to be a writer. If I couldn't ever get anything published, I wanted to be a hairdresser and create beautiful long hairstyles all day. I didn't want to be a *teacher*. In the 1950s most teachers in primary school were in their forties and fifties, even sixties. Many of the women had their grey hair scraped back in buns. They all wore sensible flat laced shoes. When they sat down, their long-legged pink directoire knickers showed unless they kept their knees clamped together. I didn't want to look like a teacher.

I was glad to see the back of the Bump Man. To cheer me up Biddy took me to the Book Corner. There, sitting on a chair, was the famous children's writer Pamela Brown. We knew it was her because she had a placard saying so right above her head. She looked incredibly smart and glamorous, the exact opposite of a frumpy teacher. She was dressed all in black, wearing a beautifully cut black tailored suit, a tiny black feathery hat on her soft curls, and high-heeled black suede shoes. She wore a string of pearls round her neck, one last elegant touch.

She was sitting bolt upright on her chair, staring straight ahead. I know now the poor woman must have been dying of embarrassment, stuck there all alone, waiting for someone, *anyone*, to approach her, but to me then she seemed like a queen on her throne. I just wanted to gaze at her reverently.

Biddy had other ideas. She prodded me in the back.

'Go and say hello to her then!' she said.

'I can't!' I mouthed.

'Yes you can! It's Pamela Brown. You know, you like her books.'

Of course I knew.

'So *tell* her you like them,' said Biddy.

I was almost as frightened of Pamela Brown as

I was of George Cansdale, but at least she was unlikely to produce a snake from her handbag and wrap it round my neck.

'Hello,' I whispered, approaching her.

'Hello,' said Pamela Brown.

She seemed a little at a loss for words too but she smiled at me very sweetly.

'I like your books,' I confided.

'I'm so pleased,' she said.

We smiled some more and then I backed away, both of us sighing with relief.

> *Who's got a worst enemy called Moyra*
> *who had a gigantic snake called Crusher*
> *for a pet?*

It's Verity in *The Cat Mummy*.

Do you have any pets? My best friend Sophie has got four kittens called Sporty, Scary, Baby and Posh. My second-best friend Laura has a golden Labrador dog called Dustbin. My sort-of-boyfriend Aaron has got a dog too, a black mongrel called Liquorice Allsorts, though he gets called Licky for short. My worst enemy Moyra has got a boa constrictor snake called Crusher. Well, she says she has. I've never been to her house so I don't know if she's telling fibs.

I've got a very sweet-natured elderly ginger and white cat called Whisky. I wouldn't mind a kitten and I'd love a dog – but I would *hate* to have any kind of snake as a pet!

23

More Books!

I don't apologize for another chapter about books (and it's a long one too). This is a book *about* books. I wouldn't be a writer now if I hadn't been a reader.

I've told you about my two favourite books, *Nancy and Plum* and *Adventures with Rosalind*, but I'm afraid you can't read them for yourself because they're long out of print. I've mentioned Enid Blyton and Eve Garnett and Pamela Brown, but I think my favourite popular contemporary author was Noel Streatfeild.

Her most famous book is *Ballet Shoes*, a lovely story about three adopted sisters, Pauline, Petrova and Posy Fossil, who attend a stage school. Pauline wants to be an actress, Petrova aches to be an airline pilot and Posy is already a brilliant ballet dancer. *I* wanted to be a ballet dancer too. I loved dancing and could pick up little routines quite quickly. I had read enough books about girls longing to be dancers to realize that I had ballet dancer's *feet*. My second toe is longer than my big toe, which means I could go up on my points more easily, and

I have very high arches. I was sure this was a genuine sign that I could be a Belle of the Ballet. I wanted most of all to be a writer, of course, but I didn't see why I couldn't be a ballet dancer too. Ann Taylor did ballet. Mandy did ballet.

'Well, *you're* not doing ballet,' said Biddy. 'I'm not tackling those costumes. It would be a bally nightmare.' She chuckled at her own bad joke.

Biddy had done ballet herself as a small child. She was little and cute with curly hair so she'd been chosen to be in all the concerts, as a fairy, a kitten, a rabbit . . . Ga had made all her costumes.

'We can't ask her to make your costumes now her arthritis is so bad,' Biddy said firmly. 'You wouldn't *like* ballet anyway. You wouldn't be any good at it. *I* wasn't.'

So I never got to try. I practised valiantly by myself for a while. I had a pair of pale pink pull-on bedroom slippers and I pretended these were proper ballet shoes. When Biddy and Harry were at work, I hummed the 'Sugar Plum Fairy' tune and pranced up and down our flat, whirling and twirling round the table and the television, pirouetting down the hall, executing a daring leap up onto Biddy's bed and then sweeping a deep ballerina curtsey to myself in her dressing-table mirror. Perhaps it's just as well I didn't have an audition.

I picked up a lot of tips from *Ballet Shoes* but

most of all I liked it for all the realistic little details of girl life. It was written in the 1930s so it was already dated when I read it twenty years later. I puzzled over the Fossil sisters' poverty when they lived in a huge house on the Cromwell Road and had a cook and a nanny, but I loved it that they were such *real* girls. They quarrelled and larked around and worried about things. I felt they were *my* sisters. I sighed over Pauline becoming swollen-headed when she had her first big part in a play; I suffered agonies with Petrova, forced into acting when she felt such a fool on stage and longed to be with Mr Simpson fixing cars in his garage; I envied Posy as she glided through life, showing off and being insufferably cute. I knew how important it was for the girls to have a smart black velvet frock for their auditions. I loved the necklaces they got for a Christmas present from Great-uncle Matthew. I longed to go too on their seaside holiday to Pevensey. I knew without being told that it was definitely a cut above Clacton.

Noel Streatfeild was a prolific writer, and so I went backwards and forwards to the library, determined to read everything she'd ever written. I owned *Ballet Shoes*. It was one of the early Puffin books, with a bright green cover and Ruth Gervis's pleasing pictures of the three girls in ballet dresses on the front. Those illustrations seemed so much part of the whole book (Ruth Gervis was Noel

Streatfeild's sister) that the modern un-illustrated versions all seem to have an important part lacking. But at least *Ballet Shoes* is still in print. Most of Noel Streatfeild's books have long since disappeared from bookshops and libraries.

I loved *White Boots* and *Tennis Shoes* and *Curtain Up*. I was given *Wintle's Wonders* as a summer holiday present. I remember clutching it to my chest so happily the edges poked me through my thin cotton dress. It was an agreeably chunky book, which meant it might last me several days.

Noel Streatfeild edited a very upmarket magazine for children called the *Elizabethan*, which I subscribed to. Enid Blyton had a magazine too, *Sunny Stories*, but that was very much for younger children. I had to struggle hard with some of the uplifting erudite articles in the *Elizabethan*, which was strange because Noel's books were wonderfully easy to read.

She wrote some fascinating volumes of autobiography, and one biography of *her* favourite children's writer, E. Nesbit.

I loved E. Nesbit too. Biddy gave me *The Story of the Treasure Seekers* when I was seven. It was my first classic but it wasn't too difficult for me as it was written in the first person. You were meant to guess which one of the Bastable children was the narrator. It seemed pretty obvious to me that it was Oswald. I didn't realize this was all part of the joke. Now I think *The Story of the Treasure Seekers* is a very warm and witty book, and it makes me crack up laughing, but as a seven-year-old I took it very seriously indeed. It seemed perfectly possible to me that the children *might* find a fortune. I failed to understand that Albert's uncle frequently helped them out. I had no idea that if you added several spoonfuls of sugar to sherry, it would taste disgusting. I'd had a sip of Ga's Harvey's Bristol Cream at Christmas and thought it was even worse than Gongon's black treacle medicine. *I* thought the taste would be improved with a liberal sprinkling of sugar too.

I wished there were more Bastable *girls*. I liked Alice a lot, and I felt sorry for poor po-faced Dora, especially when she wept and told Oswald she tried so hard to keep her brothers and sister in order because their dying mother had asked her to look after the family. There were occasional Edwardian references that I didn't understand. I sniggered at the boys wearing garments called knickerbockers. But E. Nesbit's writing style was so lively and child-friendly, and the children seemed so real that I felt I was a token Treasure Seeker too, especially as they lived in Lewisham.

I loved *The Railway Children* too, and was particularly fond of Bobbie. I liked it that Mother was a writer and whenever she sold a story, there were buns for tea. (I copied this idea many years later whenever *I* sold a story to a publisher!) There was a special children's serial of *The Railway Children* on television – not the lovely film starring Jenny Agutter, this was many years earlier than that.

I sat in front of our new television set, spellbound. At the end of each episode the television announcer said a few words. She was called Jennifer, a smiley, wavy-haired girl who was only about twelve. She told all the child viewers about a *Railway Children* art competition.

'All you have to do is illustrate your favourite scene,' she said, smiling straight at me, cross-legged on the living-room floor in Cumberland House.

'Mummy, can I do some painting?' I said.

I had to ask permission because Biddy wasn't keen on me having my painting water on the dining table and went through an elaborate performance of covering it over with newpapers, and rolling my sleeves right up to my elbows so my cuffs wouldn't get smudged with wet watercolour.

'Of course you're not doing any painting now. You're due for bed in ten minutes,' said Biddy.

She believed in Early Nights, even though I'd often lie awake for hours.

'But it's for a competition on the television,' I said. *'Please!'*

Biddy considered. I was quite good at painting for my age. Most of the children in the Infants were still at the big-blob combined-head-and-body stage, with stick arms and legs, the sky a blue stripe at the top of the page and the grass a green stripe at the bottom. I'd copied so many pictures out of my books that I had a slightly more sophisticated style, and I liked giving all my faces elaborate features. I was a dab hand at long eyelashes, though I was sometimes too enthusiastic, so my people looked as if two tarantulas had crawled onto each face.

'Have a go then,' said Biddy, relenting.

I was still having a go when Harry came home from work wanting his tea.

'You'll have to wait for once,' said Biddy. 'Jac's painting.'

I dabbled my paintbrush and daubed proudly. I was on my third attempt. I'd tried hard to draw a train for my first picture, but I couldn't work out what they looked like. I didn't have any books with trains in them. I'd seen the little blue *Thomas The Tank Engine* books in W. H. Smith's, but I didn't fancy them as a girly read.

I made a determined attempt at a train, painting it emerald-green, but it looked like a giant caterpillar. I took another piece of paper and tried to draw the train head-on, but I couldn't work out where the wheels went, and I'd used up so much green paint already there was just a dab left in my Reeves paintbox.

'Blow the train,' I muttered. I drew Bobbie and Phyllis and Peter instead, frantically waving red flannel petticoats. I drew them as if *I* was the train, rapidly approaching them. Their faces reflected this, their mouths crimson Os as they screamed.

I got a bit carried away with the high drama of it all, sloshing on the paint so vigorously that it started to run and I had to blot it up hurriedly with my cuddle hankie. The finished painting was a little wrinkly but I still felt it was quite good.

'Put your name and address on the back carefully,' said Biddy. 'And put your age.'

I did as I was told and she sent it off to the television studio at Alexandra Palace the next day.

I won in my age category! It was the only time I won anything as a child. They didn't send my painting back, which was a pity, but they sent a Rowney drawing pad as a prize. I've felt very fond of *The Railway Children* ever since.

I'd read my way through most of the girly children's classics before I was ten. Woolworths used to stock garishly produced, badly printed children's classics for 2s 6d, a third of the price of most modern books. I read *Little Women* over and over again, loving Jo, the tomboy harem-scarem sister who read voraciously and was desperate to be a writer. I also had a soft spot for Beth because she was shy and liked playing with dolls. I loved *What Katy Did* and felt desperately sorry for poor little Elsie, the middle child who wasn't in on Katy and Clover's secrets. I wasn't so interested in Katy after she fell off the swing and endured her long illness. I couldn't stomach saintly Cousin Helen. I enjoyed the Christmas chapter the most, and the detailed descriptions of all the presents.

I read *The Secret Garden* by Frances Hodgson Burnett, thrilled to read about irritable, spoiled children for a change, totally understanding *why* they behaved badly. I liked *A Little Princess* even more. I found Sara Crewe a magical character. I particularly loved the part at the beginning where she finds her doll Emily and there's a detailed description of her trunk of clothes. I shivered in the attic with Sara after her fortune changed, and found the scenes with Becky and Ermengarde very touching. I was charmed that Sara made a pet out of Melchisedec – though if a real rat had scampered across the carpet in my bedroom, I'd have screamed my head off.

I read the beginning of *Jane Eyre* too. Biddy had a little red leatherette copy in the bookcase. I fingered my way through many of these books, but they were mostly dull choices for a child. *Jane Eyre* was in very small print, uncomfortable to read, but I found the first page so riveting I carried on and on. I was there with Jane on the window seat, staring out at the rain. I felt a thrill of recognition when she described poring over the illustrations in Bewick's *History of British Birds*. I trembled when her cousins tormented her. I was horrified when Jane's aunt had the servants haul her off to the terrifying Red Room. I shivered with Jane when she was sent to the freezing cold Lowood boarding school. I burned with humiliation when she was forced to stand in disgrace with the slate saying LIAR! around her neck. I wanted to be friends with clever odd Helen Burns too. I wanted to clasp her in my arms when she was sick and dying.

I read those first few chapters again and again – and Jane joined my increasingly large cast of imaginary friends.

Which girl in my books has Jane Eyre for her imaginary friend?

It's Prue in *Love Lessons*.

For years and years I'd had a private pretend friend, an interesting and imaginative girl my own age called Jane. She started when I read the first few chapters of *Jane Eyre*. She stepped straight out of the pages and into my head. She no longer led her own Victorian life with her horrible aunt and cousins. She shared my life with my demented father.

Jane was better than a real sister. She wasn't babyish and boring like Grace. We discussed books and pored over pictures and painted watercolours together, and we talked endlessly about everything.

I didn't base the character of Prue on myself, even though we shared an imaginary friend *and* both had odd fathers. I was quite good at art, like Prue, and I was also fond of an interesting Polish art teacher at secondary school – but I *didn't* fall in love with him!

24

Television and Radio

How many television channels can you watch on your set at home? How many channels do you think there were when I was a child? One! The dear old BBC – and in those days children's television lasted one hour, from five to six. That was your lot.

I watched Muffin the Mule, a shaky little puppet who trotted across the top of a piano, strings very visible. He nodded and shook his head and did a camp little hoof-prance while his minder, Annette Mills, sang, '*We love Muffin, Muffin the Mule. Dear old Muffin, playing the fool. We love Muffin – everybody sing, WE LOVE MUFFIN THE MULE.*'

Children's television was not sophisticated in those days.

Annette Mills's speciality was performing with puppets. She also did a little weekly show with Prudence Kitten. I *adored* Prudence. She was a black cat glove puppet, ultra girly, who wore flouncy frocks and pinafores. You couldn't get colour television in those days so I always had to guess the colour of Prudence's frocks. She had her own little kitchen and bustled around baking cakes and making cups of tea, especially when her best friend Primrose was coming on a visit.

There was another puppet on children's television called Mr Turnip, an odd little man with a turnip head. He was best buddies with a real man called Humphrey Lestocq. No one could spell his name so viewers were encouraged to call him H.L. when he appeared on his television programme, *Whirligig*.

There was a slapstick comedian specially for children called Mr Pastry, a doddery old man who kept tripping over and making lots of mess. Comedians on adult television weren't necessarily more inspiring, though Biddy and Harry and I laughed at Arthur Askey, especially when he did his 'Busy Bee' song (don't ask!), and Harry had a soft spot for Benny Hill.

Television went wildly upmarket and downmarket, in those days. There was *The Brains Trust*, with its bombastic introductory music and its little quote from Alexander Pope: 'To speak his thought is every human's right.' Even panel games were treated very seriously. We watched *What's My Line?* every week, hosted by Eamonn Andrews (chatty Irishman), with Lady Isobel Barnett (posh dark-haired lady), Barbara Kelly (lively Canadian blonde), David Nixon (bald magician) and Gilbert Harding (grumpy intellectual). Eamonn and David and Gilbert wore full evening dress with bow ties; Lady Isobel and Barbara wore long dresses with straps and sweetheart necklines.

Some of the children's programmes were posh classy affairs too. Huw Wheldon had a talent show for children called *All Your Own*. He seldom chose showy little singers and dancers with ringlets and toothy grins. Huw Wheldon specialized in pale spectacled geeky children with high-pitched voices who played the cello or collected stamps. There was once a glorious troupe of strange children who acted out a mad chess game, singing at the end, *'Ro, ro, rolio, tumpty tumpty tum. Now the battle's over, we'll have lots of fun!'*

ITV started up when I was about eight but Biddy fought not to have it. She said it was common. Maybe we simply couldn't afford a new television set. Everyone at school was talking about all the new programmes, especially *Wagon Train*.

'Silly cowboy rubbish,' said Biddy, sniffing.

Then she weakened, or maybe Harry forked out so he could watch his horse-racing on the new channel. We had a brand-new television with a fourteen-inch screen – and ITV. I *still* wasn't able to join in the *Wagon Train* discussions at school. We watched one episode and Biddy poured scorn on it. It wasn't just silly cowboys, it was *sentimental*. Biddy said it made her want to throw up.

I was sometimes allowed to watch cowboys on children's television: the Lone Ranger with his trusty friend Tonto – or was that his horse? No, that was Silver. You saw him rearing up at the start of the show, the masked Lone Ranger waving on his back. I didn't like cowboys particularly, I just liked the part where they moseyed into town and stomped bow-legged into the saloon bar. I longed to be one of the naughty ladies who ran the saloon. I loved their flouncy ruffled skirts and their fancy high-heeled cowboy boots. There was also Davy Crockett with his furry hat. For a while every small boy wanted one of those hats with a weird tail hanging down the back. They all hid round corners and fired at each other with their toy Davy Crockett guns. He had his own theme tune: '*Davy – Daveee Crockett, King of the Wild Frontier.*'

This was always requested on *Children's Favourites* on a Saturday morning, which was on the radio. Practically every child in the country listened to Uncle Mac and the selection for each Saturday. He rarely played the current favourites in the Hit Parade. These were special *children's* songs, played over and over again throughout the fifties. The lyrics themselves were repetitious:

How much is that doggy in the window?
(Woof, woof!)

The one with the waggly tail.
How much is that doggy in the window?
(Woof, woof!)
I do hope that doggy's for sale.

How about:

> *There's a tiny house*
> *(There's a tiny house)*
> *By a tiny stream,*
> *(By a tiny stream,)*
> *Where a lovely lass*
> *(Where a lovely lass)*
> *Had a lovely dream,*
> *(Had a lovely dream,)*
> *And her dream came true*
> *Quite unexpectedly*
> *In Gilly Gilly Ossenfeffer Katzenellen*
> *Bogen by the Sea.*

That was sung with great gusto by Max
Bygraves, who recorded any number of comedy
songs. I was very fond of his 'Pink Toothbrush'
song, which always made me laugh.

Best of all was 'Nellie the Elephant' – by Mandy
Miller! Mandy had made records before. They were
dire – even I had to admit it, though I still loved
playing them on our wind-up gramophone. We

owned very few records. Harry liked Mantovani, and we had the soundtrack to *South Pacific*, and the Mandy recordings. Mandy's best effort so far had been singing, '*Oh let the world be full of sunshine, for Mummy, for Daddy and for me.*' She didn't always stay in tune either. But she really came into her own when she made 'Nellie the Elephant'. It was a sweet, funny song with a proper story and she sang it beautifully, putting her heart and soul into it, going, '*Trumpety trump trump trump!*' with great emphasis and expression.

Which of my characters gets to appear in a Children of Courage *documentary on television?*

It's Elsa in *The Bed and Breakfast Star*.

My news interview was repeated later in the year in a special compilation programme called *Children of Courage*. And I got to do another interview with a nice blonde lady with big teeth, and Mum spent some of Mack's betting money on a beautiful new outfit from the Flowerfields Shopping Centre for my special telly appearance.

I've been on television lots of times now. I'm especially proud that I've got a gold Blue Peter badge! I think my favourite time was when *The South Bank Show* did a documentary about me. They didn't just interview me – my daughter Emma's on the programme too, and my dear friend Anne, and there's even a glimpse of my best secondary school friend Chris. Paterson, the jeweller who makes all my wonderful rings, says on the programme that 'Jacky's rock 'n' roll!' I loved that bit.

I've also been on *Desert Island Discs* on the radio, which was great fun. My first choice of music was . . . 'Nellie the Elephant'!

25

Teachers

The head of Latchmere Juniors was a man called Mr Pearson. I have a photo of me standing next to him but I don't think I ever spoke more than a couple of sentences to him. We weren't frightened of him though. He seemed a quiet, kind, gentle man, though every now and then he caned one of the boys in Prayers. I always shut my eyes when this happened. Mr Pearson didn't seem to have much stomach for corporal punishment either, and got it over and done with as briskly as possible.

He spoke earnestly in Prayers, often telling us inspirational true-life stories (like the ones on the back of my *Girl* comic). He had a particular passion for Shackleton and told us such vivid stories about his long trek across the ice that we shivered even in the height of summer.

Mr Pearson was a chess fanatic too and insisted that every child in the Juniors be taught how to play. There was a special chess club, and children were always to be found sitting cross-legged in the playground around a chessboard. I learned to play too but I wasn't very good at it. I didn't have a mathematical mind that could plan ahead. I couldn't apply my mind to plotting potential chess moves. I'd think *castle* and *knight* and I'd be off in a daydream, galloping the little wooden knight through imaginary forests to an enchanted castle. My king would be in check before I knew where I was.

Mr Pearson took us for a lesson when we were in the top class, our equivalent of Year Six. He taught us *codes* – how to invent them and how to crack them. I was better at this. I knew the shape of words, the rhythm of a sentence, and often worked by instinct rather than patient analysis. I should have taken up writing in code. Years later I stupidly confided all sorts of secret things to my diary. Biddy read it and hit the roof – and the floor – and all four walls.

Our form teachers taught us English and arithmetic and PT. We had a special teacher, Miss Audric, who taught us scripture, music and nature study. Most of the teachers were eccentric. Miss Audric was the all-time Queen of Quirkiness. She had bright carrot-coloured hair wound in plaits round her head. On sunny summer days she'd sit in the grass quadrangle, undo her hair and brush it out so that it fell in an orange curtain way past her waist. Then she'd plait it all up again, playing Rapunzel. She wore woollen suits, hand-crocheted, in extraordinary bright colours – emerald green, purple, electric blue. She played the violin and the piano and all different kinds of recorder. She winced when we had difficulty piping our way accurately through 'Little Bird'. She was someone else who believed she had a personal hotline to Jesus. She told us stories about him as if he was a dear friend of hers. We almost believed she'd nipped on a bus to visit her pal when he was sharing out the loaves and fishes and raising Lazarus from the dead.

I always had problems with Jesus' miracles. I could *believe* them, but didn't see how they worked. I thought of those five loaves and two small fishes. I thought of five sandwich loaves. What kind of fish would you find in the sea of Galilee? Cod? If Jesus was holy enough to spread this simple feast around five thousand hungry people, why didn't he pull out all the stops and provide chips to go with the fish, and maybe mushy peas too, and some butter to go on the bread? Then I had problems with Lazarus, resurrected from the tomb, smelling so bad that all the disciples had to put their sleeves over their noses so they didn't breathe in his decaying stench. What happened *next*? Did poor Lazarus have to trail around Palestine with his reek all around him, shunned by everyone? Did he look like the Living Dead from Zombie-land, creatures in an American horror comic I wasn't supposed to read?

I really wanted to know the answers to these and a host of other biblical questions, but I had enough sense not to ask Miss Audric. She was very strict and could quell you with one of her looks. If you got the giggles during one of her squawky violin solos, then Woe Betide You.

Miss Audric had a mad dog that thought it was a wolf. Whenever she took it for walks in Richmond Park, it made a beeline for the deer. The herd scattered as it raced up, teeth bared. Even the mightiest stag would trot off in terror. Miss Audric's dog could probably see off a herd of elephants, let alone timid deer. She brought it to school occasionally and we were all scared stiff of it. I can't remember what it was really called but we all nicknamed it Fang.

Miss Audric decided to take us on a walk in Richmond Park for our nature study lesson. She rounded us all up – more than forty of us – made us form a crocodile, then marched us out of the school and up to the park. This was a brisk half-hour walk in itself. Many of us were flagging by the time we got to the park gates. Still, it was a sunny day and we went whooping and swooping into the ferny wilderness of Richmond Park, dodging around the ancient oak trees.

Miss Audric didn't stop us. We were all escapees

from school now. It was time to go back for the next lesson but Miss Audric didn't care. She strode out in her conker-coloured lace-ups and we skipped after her.

We went past the witch's pond, further into the park than I'd ever been with Harry, up and over the steep hill, across the flat plain where the deer grazed. Miss Audric lectured us on the differences between red deer and fallow deer and taught us about antler formation. Some of the boys raised their arms and pretended to be stags, locking antlers. We were all getting a bit restless now.

'Miss Audric, it's getting very *late*,' Cherry interrupted nervously.

She learned the violin and was Miss Audric's favourite.

'Well, we can all go scurrying straight back to school – *or* we can fill our lungs with this fine fresh air and finish our lovely walk,' said Miss Audric. 'Hands up who wants to keep on walking!'

We were all tired out by this time but none of us was brave enough to keep our hands down. We waved in the air and feigned enthusiasm and we walked on . . . and on . . . and on, all the way to Pen Ponds. We couldn't help perking up then because the two vast ponds shone blue in the sunlight. They had bright yellow sand at the edge, just like the seaside. Seagulls circled overhead and ducks and swans bobbed up and down on little waves.

Miss Audric sat regally on a bench, taking off her shoes *and* her lisle stockings. She undid them decorously, manipulating her suspenders through her crocheted skirt, but it still seemed very bold of her. We kept giving her long pale feet little sideways glances. Miss Audric wriggled her toes, perfectly content.

We begged to go paddling.

'Just get your tootsies wet – and no splashing!' she commanded.

The girls teetered at the edge, obediently only ankle-deep. The boys plunged in up to their scabby knees, holding their trousers up to their groin. There was a *lot* of splashing.

'Behave yourselves!' Miss Audric bellowed, but she still didn't sound cross.

It was as if we were in a fairytale place and Miss Audric was turning into an unlikely wood nymph. She let down her long hair and stretched out in the sunshine. She closed her eyes. She wasn't falling asleep, was she? It was getting very very late. We wouldn't be back for the end of afternoon school at this rate.

Cherry cleared her throat. 'What's the time, Miss Audric?' she said loudly.

We peered at Miss Audric nervously, as if she might turn into a wolf and yell *Dinner time*! She did look annoyed to be woken from her nap, but when she consulted her watch, she seemed a little startled.

'Shoes and socks on, lickety-spit,' she said, rolling up her stockings and fitting them carefully over her feet and up her long pale legs. She didn't seem to mind not having a towel to dry herself. We all had to cope without one too, though it was horrible squeezing soaking wet sandy feet into tight socks and shoes.

'Right, back through the park, quick *march*!' said Miss Audric.

We weren't up to marching now. We could barely crawl. Our wet socks rubbed our feet raw. We were all limping with blisters before we got to the park gates. Miss Audric kept checking her watch now, urging us to hurry up.

'I *can't* hurry!'

'I'm *tired*!'

'My feet are so *sore*.'

'I want to go to the toilet.'

'I want to sit *down*.'

'Yes, let's all sit down for a bit, Miss Audric, *please*.'

'No sitting! We've got to walk – *fast*! I tell you what, we'll sing.' Miss Audric threw back her head. '*I love to go a-wandering* – come on, join in, all of you!'

So we all sang.

'I love to go a-wandering
Along the mountain track,
And as I go, I love to sing,
My knapsack on my back.
Valdereeee, Valderaaaa,
Valderee, Valderaa-ha-ha-ha
My knapsack on my back!

We went a-wandering all the way back through the Kingston streets to school. Mothers were clustered anxiously in the playground. Mr Pearson was standing in the main entrance, arms folded. Miss Audric wasn't cowed. She swept past them like the Pied Piper, leading her limping bunch of children back into school.

Perhaps it was just as well Miss Audric wasn't a form teacher. She might well have abducted her class for a week at a time. Her children would have developed stout legs and stamina and known a great deal about Jesus and music and nature, but reading, writing and arithmetic wouldn't have got a look in.

Our form teachers weren't *quite* as eccentric as Miss Audric, but they were a very weird bunch all the same. The first year of the Juniors we had Mrs Dowling. She was a teacher of the old school – scraped-back bun, pleated skirt, flat lace-ups. She could be scathing at times. I wore a new dress with a flared skirt to school one day, and I couldn't resist twirling round once or twice.

'Thank you for showing us your knickers, Jacqueline,' said Mrs Dowling, and of course everyone sniggered.

We had Mrs Symons in our second year and she was so much sweeter. She was Austrian and had a heavy accent, so we thought, ignorantly, that she was a bit 'funny'. She tried very hard to make every child feel special. She liked my stories and gave me big ticks and the odd gold star, even though my pages were likely to be full of blots and smears. I had trouble with the school dipping pens. My ideas ran away with me and I couldn't write quickly with those horrible scratchy pens because the ink spurted out and spattered the page. The inkwells encouraged the boys to play *Beano*-comic tricks. They'd dunk the tips of girls' plaits in the inkwells and make inky blotting-paper pellets and fire them with their rulers.

When we were nearly at the end of term, Mrs Symons told us that Santa Claus would be coming soon. We were streetwise kids, eight going on nine. We looked at her, eyebrows raised.

'Don't you believe in Santa Claus?' said Mrs Symons, pretending to be shocked. 'You wait and see, my dears.'

On the last day Mrs Symons took the register and then told us she had to go on an errand, but a special visitor would be coming to look after us. She trotted off. Five minutes later a portly gentleman with a long white beard came striding into our classroom in wellington boots, wearing a scarlet robe edged with white cotton wool.

'Hello, children! I'm Santa Claus!' he said, with a pronounced Austrian accent.

Santa Claus was carrying a big sack. He had little wrapped presents for every single child in the class.

I loved dear Mrs Symons – but I loved my next form teacher even more.

I've written a book where a boy character likes playing chess in the playground. Which book is it – and what's the boy's name?

It's *Bad Girls* – and the boy is Mandy's friend Arthur King.

I sat next to Arthur King at lunchtime and then afterwards he tried to teach me how to play chess. It got ever so boring. I wanted to let my mind wander and think about Tanya meeting me from school and how we were going to be friends for ever and ever.

'No, *look*, if you put your queen there I'll be able to take it with my knight,' said Arthur.

I couldn't get worked up about it. The queen didn't have long hair and a flowing dress, the knight didn't have shining armour and a plume in his helmet. They were just twirly pieces of plastic with no personality whatsover.

Mandy gives Arthur rather a hard time at first. I'm glad she makes proper friends with him at the end of the book.

THE MAGGOTTS.

BY

JACQUELINE AITKEN.

26

Mr Townsend

Mr Townsend took us in the third year. I fell in love the very first day in his class. He stood in front of the blackboard and wrote his name – L. R. Townsend – in beautiful chalk copperplate. L. R. We found out soon enough that these initials stood for Leonard Reginald, dreadful old-codger names, but nothing could make Mr Townsend seem ridiculous. He wasn't a particularly tall man, but he was fit and muscular, with tanned skin and dark-blond curly hair, practically film-star looks, a world away from the usual musty male teacher model.

He smiled at us all and sat on the edge of his desk.

'Hello, everyone. I'm Mr Townsend. By the end of the day I hope I'll know all *your* names.'

We all sat up straight at our desks and smiled back at him.

'Isn't he *lovely*?' Marion whispered.

I sat next to her that year, though we didn't really have much in common. Marion was a very blonde girl with a very pink face. She looked squeaky clean, as if she'd just had a good scrub in her bath. She was squeaky clean inside too. She went to church twice on Sundays, knew her Scripture off by heart and prayed to Jesus every night. Marion had a special smug holy expression when she said the word Jesus.

I knew even on that first day that Marion and I weren't always going to see eye to eye, but at least we were united in our love for Mr Townsend. There wasn't a single child who didn't adore him. The boys loved him because he was sporty. He still played for a good rugby team and he loved cricket and tennis. He encouraged the athletic boys and coached them enthusiastically, but he didn't shout at the weedy ones who ran knock-kneed and couldn't catch. He was gently sympathetic – but he was no easy pushover. He never let anyone take advantage of his good nature. He never caned any child. He didn't need to. The girls loved him because he was so kind and caring and artistic too. He shyly showed us his watercolour sketchbook. We all tried hard to copy his delicate landscapes with the school primary colour poster paints.

He taught us our lessons, fairly but firmly, but at play times he wasn't just our teacher, he was our friend. He'd throw a ball about with the boys and ruffle their hair and pretend to bop them on the nose. He'd chat to the girls, treating us totally seriously. A little bunch of us would lean against him fondly. Marion once actually climbed on his knee. There was never anything odd or weird about Mr Townsend. We all knew adults who'd try to pat you or cuddle you too close. Mr Townsend was as kindly and gentle and safe as Santa Claus, though he didn't have a silly beard or a habit of going 'Ho ho ho!'

I tried harder in his lessons than I ever had before, simply because I wanted to be top of his class. I didn't have much chance because I was totally useless at arithmetic. I could add and subtract and multiply and divide accurately enough (though I frequently had to work it out on my fingers), but I couldn't do *problems*. You know the sort of thing: *If it takes six men ten days to dig a hole 30 feet by 60 feet how long will it take eight men?* I couldn't concentrate on the logistics. I made up the six men in my head and wondered *why* they were digging this hole of such huge dimensions. Was it the foundations of a house? A swimming pool? A grave for an elephant? What time in the morning did they start digging? Did they have breaks for a cup of tea and a bacon sandwich? Why were the two extra men brought into play? Were they reserve builders, like reserve players in a football match? I'd be off in a daydream and all the other children would be on question three already. Marion was good at arithmetic. It was her second-best subject (she shone at scripture). When we had an arithmetic test, I edged a little closer to her at our shared desk. She hunched over her page as she wrote down her sums, guarding her work with her hand, but as she turned the page, I could sometimes get a glimpse of her neat answers.

She saw me writing down an answer at the end of my untidy workings out and frowned. 'You copied that off me!' she whispered.

My mouth went dry. I suppose I *had* copied. Copycats were deeply despised.

'No I didn't,' I said.

'That's a fib!' said Marion.

'No, I didn't copy, I *didn't*,' I lied.

I was getting scared Marion might tell Mr Townsend. I glanced at him anxiously.

Marion saw me looking. 'I'm not a telltale,' she said.

'There's nothing to tell because I didn't copy, so there,' I said.

'I know you did,' said Marion. She paused. 'And *Jesus* knows too!'

I couldn't help looking up to see if I could spot Jesus peering all the way down from Heaven, sucking his teeth and shaking his head at me. But at least Mr Townsend didn't know, and I cared about him much more than I did about Marion's Jesus.

I managed to pass muster in all the other

lessons. I shone at English. I liked it best when we could make up stories, but I tried hard when we were told to write factual accounts too. Sometimes I blurred the distinction between the two. Mr Townsend set us the subject 'My Day Out'.

I chewed the top of my pen, deliberating. Marion set to work, scribbling away with her fountain pen, writing about her day out in the country in Daddy's Morris Minor. It was all right for her. We didn't have a car so we didn't have Days Out. We hardly ever went out as a family, Biddy, Harry and me. It wouldn't work – Biddy would nag and bicker, Harry would snap and sulk, I'd pick my hangnails and start pretending.

Well, I could *pretend* a Day Out, couldn't I? I got cracking with a sigh of relief. I decided we'd go for a Day Out in London. I didn't invent a posh car for us. I wanted to be convincing. I took us by train from Kingston railway station. I embellished the journey with a few imaginary treats. I had a *Girl* comic and a packet of Spangles to suck while Mummy and Daddy chatted and laughed and looked out of the window.

I knew what to do with us when we got to Waterloo. We went over the bridge to the Strand. I was proud of my authentic details. I walked us up the Charing Cross Road to Foyles. I knew this was the biggest bookshop in London. I had several books at home with the distinctive green Foyles sticker inside. I described my book-browsing session in loving detail, fantasizing about the different books in the children's section. I decided Mummy would buy me *What Katy Did at School* and Daddy would buy me *Tennis Shoes* by Noel Streatfeild.

Then we went to Hamleys, the big toyshop in Regent Street. I looked at the dolls with Mummy and the toy trains with Daddy, and they bought me a tiny teapot no bigger than my thumbnail for my doll's house. Then we had lunch at Lyons Corner House, the only restaurant I knew in London.

I had another gnaw of my pen, deliberating over our afternoon. I decided we'd go to the zoo. I'd been there once when I was five to see baby Brumus, the polar bear, so this pretend time we went to see Brumus grown up, and the monkeys and the lions and the giraffes. I had a ride on a camel and an elephant. This wasn't fantasy – children really could have special rides on the animals in those days. It had actually been very uncomfortable on that baby Brumus visit. I'd been placed between the camel's humps and I was scared I might slip sideways. You sat on a special seat for the elephant ride, but I'd been strapped in with a lot of over-excited boys who kept poking me, and they all shrieked with laughter and said rude things when the elephant relieved itself.

I walked us all round the zoo, Biddy and Harry and I all licking Wall's ice-cream wafers. Biddy wasn't a woman who'd willingly walk to the end of the road in her tiny size-three heels, and she actively disliked most animals, so my imaginative powers were stretched to the limit.

I let us all have a sit down and *another* slap-up meal in Lyons. Our Day Out wasn't over yet. I extended it into the evening. I decided to take us to the cinema to see a film called *The Bad Seed*.

Biddy and Harry had actually seen this film when it was on in Kingston. I'd longed to see it. I'd seen stills from the film in *Picturegoer*, a magazine I bought every now and then in case it had photos of Mandy. *The Bad Seed* starred another child film star, Patty McCormack. My heart still belonged to Mandy, but I did fall in love with Patty McCormack's wonderful ash-blonde hair, styled in a fringe at the front and then two long beautiful plaits. She looked incredibly sweet and innocent and childish, with her neat hair and checked frock and little red tap shoes. It was a thrilling shock to read a paragraph about this new film and find that Patty played a child murderer.

I begged Biddy to take me to see the film but she said it wasn't suitable. After she'd seen it herself I made her tell me all about this little girl

Rhoda, who drowned a boy in her class because he beat her in a spelling test. He was in a pond and he struggled hard to haul himself out, but Rhoda took off her tap shoe and *hammered his fingers* so he had to let go. This appalled and impressed me. Ann was the only girl I knew who wore tap shoes, and she was a sweet kind girl and one of my friends – but I decided not to argue with her all the same.

I wrote about Biddy and Harry and me going to see *The Bad Seed*. I recounted the plot at length. I'd listened avidly to Biddy. Every now and then I embellished or invented, as always.

'We all agreed it was the best film we'd ever seen. It was the end of a perfect day out,' I wrote, finishing just as the bell went.

'You've written *heaps*,' said Marion, comparing her sparse page and a half with my six, seven, *eight* pages.

I shrugged modestly. I might be rubbish at maths, but I could certainly write.

I hoped Mr Townsend would like my composition. When Biddy asked me if I'd had a good day at school, I told her I'd written the longest composition ever.

'What was the subject?' Biddy asked, as she peeled the potatoes for our favourite treat supper, roast pork chops.

'"My Day Out",' I said, starting to shell the peas for her. I loved doing this and helping myself to the tiny peas in the flat pods – but I always jumped if I found a maggot.

'Mm,' said Biddy absent-mindedly, slicing the potatoes and arranging them in the roasting tin. 'So what did you write about? Did you tell about the time I got you all the Mandy photos in Wardour Street?'

'No, I forgot. I did put about looking at the dolls in Hamleys though,' I said.

'Did you say I bought you those Old Cottage dolls?'

'Well, no, you didn't buy them with me on a day out – they were my Christmas present,' I said.

Biddy raised her eyebrows at me and shoved the roasting tin in the oven. She started shelling peas too.

'You could have juggled with the facts a little to make a good story,' she said. 'You *love* your dolls. And they cost a fortune.'

'Yes, well, I put a lot else. I said you gave me lots of treats – and we all went to *The Bad Seed* in the evening,' I said.

Biddy jumped as if she'd found a maggot as big as a snake. 'You said I took you to *The Bad Seed*!' she said.

'You and me and Daddy,' I said.

'But we *didn't* take you!'

'Yes, I know, but I was juggling with the facts to make a good story,' I said, echoing her exactly.

This was not a wise plan. She thought I was being deliberately cheeky and gave me a good shake.

'How on *earth* could you put such a stupid thing? As if I'd ever take you to a film like that. Did you say what it was *about*?'

'Yes, I told the whole story,' I said, my head juddering. 'All about Rhoda and the little boy and the tap shoes and how she killed him.'

'You stupid *idiot*!' said Biddy. 'What sort of mother will he think me, taking you to a film like that! Have you handed this composition in?'

'Yes, at the end of the lesson.'

'Then he's probably marking it right this minute,' said Biddy. 'Well, you must go and tell him first thing tomorrow morning that it was a pack of lies.'

'I can't do that!' I said, starting to cry.

'If you don't tell him, I'll come to the school and tell him myself,' said Biddy, and I knew she meant it.

I spent a sleepless night worrying about it. Mr Townsend would be so hurt and shocked when he found out I was a liar. He'd never like me again. He'd be fondest of saintly Marion, who would never ever lie.

I went to school early, feeling sick. I didn't tell Cherry why I was so quiet. I didn't try to play with Ann. I didn't bicker with Marion. I didn't giggle with any of the boys. I just stood in a corner, head bowed, fists clenched, as if I was already wearing a placard round my neck proclaiming me a LIAR.

Mr Townsend strode in cheerily, swinging his briefcase. He sat down at his desk, opened up his case and pulled out our green English notebooks.

My stomach lurched. I wondered if I ought to make a dash for the toilets. Mr Townsend looked up and saw me gulping like a goldfish.

'Are you all right, Jacky?' he said.

'Yes. No. I don't know,' I mumbled. I took a deep breath. 'Have you marked our English compositions yet, Mr Townsend?'

'Yes, I have.' He beckoned me closer. 'I thought yours was particularly interesting, Jacky. Well done.'

Any other time I'd have spread my wings and flown round the classroom at such sweet praise. But now I felt I was falling. I was going down down down through the parquet flooring, through all the layers of earth we'd learned about in geography, until I tumbled into Hell itself, where I belonged.

'I've got to tell you something awful, Mr Townsend,' I whispered.

'And what's that?' he said, his head on one side.

'It wasn't *true*, my Day Out,' I said. 'We didn't

go to London and we didn't go to Foyles and Hamleys and Lyons Corner House and London Zoo.'

'Didn't you?' said Mr Townsend.

'It was all lies. And . . . and . . . and I definitely didn't go to *The Bad Seed*. Mummy says she'd never take me to a film like that. I just made it all up.'

'Very convincingly,' said Mr Townsend.

He didn't sound too shocked or horrified. He looked as if he was trying not to laugh!

'So did you believe it all?' I asked.

'Well, not quite all of it,' said Mr Townsend. 'I rather think *The Bad Seed* is X-certificated. I don't suppose they'd have let a nine-year-old go into the cinema.'

'Oh,' I said. 'Mr Townsend, are you cross with me for telling lies?'

'I don't think you were really lying, Jacky. You were just making things up. There's a big difference. You've got a very vivid imagination.'

I took the deepest breath in all the world. 'Do you think I might be able to write stories one day?' I asked.

'I'm sure you will,' said Mr Townsend solemnly.

I wanted to throw my arms round his neck and kiss him.

A week or so later Mr Townsend suggested we all might like to start a special project for English.

'I'm going to give each of you your own notebook,' he said.

He patted a pile of brand-new green exercise books. School stationery was in short supply. We were taught to fill in every single line in our exercise books, even using up the fuzzy backing to the covers. We had to keep dipping our scratchy school pens far down into a thick gravy of congealed ink before we were allowed to top up our inkwells. Now we were being given a whole new notebook each. It was a sign that Mr Townsend was taking this special project seriously.

'What is our project going to be on, Mr Townsend?' Julian asked eagerly.

He was the class swot, a highly intelligent, sweet, tufty-haired boy who waved his arm all the time in the classroom, asking endless questions and knowing all the answers.

'I think I will let you all choose individual projects, Julian,' said Mr Townsend. 'I want you to write about whatever interests you most. Maybe a special sport, a hobby, a period of history, a type of animal, a favourite country – whatever you like.'

'Could I possibly do astronomy, sir?' said Julian.

A few children groaned. Other teachers would have groaned too and mocked Julian's pedantic politeness, but not Mr Townsend.

'I think that would be an excellent choice,' he said.

269

The rest of 3A had less esoteric choices.

'Bags I do football!'

'No, I'm doing football.'

'Me too.'

'Can I do rugby?'

'Can I write about my dog?'

'I want to write about France – we've been there for our holidays.'

'I want to write about birds. I've spotted heaps in my I-Spy book.'

'Can I write about Gilbert and Sullivan?' asked Cherry.

'You what?'

'Who are they?'

'Are they your boyfriends?'

'They wrote operettas. Mum and Dad sing in them and they're ever so funny,' said Cherry.

There were sniggers.

'Funny ha ha, or funny peculiar?' said Jock, screwing his finger into the side of his head to indicate loopiness.

'No, no, they *are* funny,' said Mr Townsend. '*I've* sung in *The Pirates of Penzance*, Cherry.'

This instantly gave Gilbert and Sullivan a total seal of approval.

'Please may I write about ballet?' Ann asked.

'I wonder if I could write about Jesus?' Marion asked. 'What are you going to write about, Jacky?'

'Maybe . . . maybe I could write a story?' I said.

'No, it's a *project*. You can't write an ordinary old story,' said Marion.

'Yes I can,' I said. 'Well, I don't just want to write a *story*.'

I went up to Mr Townsend's desk, not wanting to shout it out in front of all the others.

'Please could I write a novel for my project, Mr Townsend?' I said.

He hadn't mocked Julian or Cherry. He didn't mock me either.

'I think that's a brilliant idea, Jacky,' he said.

I danced back to my seat and nodded my head at Marion. 'Did you hear that? Mr Townsend said it was an excellent idea,' I said.

'He's just being kind,' said Marion. 'Anyway, you can't write a whole novel.'

'Yes I can,' I said.

I couldn't, of course. I wrote twenty-one sides, and that included a Contents page, but it was divided into seven chapters and it *seemed* like a whole novel to me.

I decided to write about a large family. I very much wanted to be a member of a large family. It was too intense when it was just Biddy and Harry and me. I decided this was going to be about a poor family with problems. I was irritated by the smug, safe, middle-class world of most of my children's books. The fathers were doctors and vicars, the mothers baked cakes and arranged flowers, the children went to posh schools and rode on ponies and had picnics and played jolly games.

I only knew one book about poor people, and that was *The Family from One End Street*. The family were called the Ruggles. I wanted to use a similar semi-comic name. I liked listening to a comedy series on the radio called *Meet the Huggetts*. I decided to call my family the Maggots. I called my first chapter 'Meet the Maggots'. My dad was called Alf and was a bus driver. I drew him with a pipe and a moustache to make it clear he was a man. I wasn't very good at drawing males.

My mum was called Daisy. She didn't go out to work, she just (!) looked after her seven children. She had a bun and worry lines across her forehead. She was particularly worried about her eldest, fifteen-year-old Marilyn, as she was 'dead keen on boys. And boys were dead keen on her too.' She was a pretty blonde. I drew her with ornate earrings. Pierced ears were considered 'fast' on young girls in the 1950s. I wanted Marilyn to be *very* fast.

Then there was Marlene. She was twelve and brainy. She'd passed her scholarship to the grammar school (as I was expected to do next year).

I wrote: 'Her interest is books. You can't drag her out of them.' Poor Marlene wasn't a beauty like her sister. She had a mousy ponytail and had to wear National Health glasses. I'd just started to wear glasses myself. Biddy was enormously proud of the fact that she'd paid for special fancy glasses with upswept frames. She wasn't having her daughter wearing little round pink National Health specs, thank you very much.

The third sister was called Mandy. She was ten and had big brown eyes and dark plaits and was desperate to be an actress. No prizes for guessing who I based *her* on!

Then I branched out and invented nine-year-old boy twins. There were boy twins in *The Family from One End Street* so I was obviously copying. I called my twins Marmaduke and Montague. Daisy had obvious aspirations for her first sons. Then she went on to have Melvyn, a shy, sensitive little boy who was mercilessly teased by five-year-old Marigold, the baby of the family. She was a fiesty little girl with abundant blonde curls and a misleading angelic expression.

I gave each child their own chapter, inventing little domestic scenarios, still shamelessly copying when I ran out of original ideas. Marilyn decided to dye her hair to please her boyfriend Sid and ended up with bright green locks – something very similar happened to Anne of Green Gables. The twins discovered stolen treasure as if they were reserve members of Enid Blyton's Famous Five.

'The Maggots' was *not* a particularly startling or stylish story, sadly – but I can nowadays claim, jokingly, that I wrote my first novel at the age of nine.

> *Who wrote a story about 'Night-time' at school and tried very hard – but her teacher said that it was very rambling, and she had a warped imagination?*

It was Tracy Beaker in the second book about her, *The Dare Game*.

Last week we had to write a story about 'Night-time' and I thought it an unusually cool subject so I wrote eight and a half pages about this girl out late at night and it's seriously spooky and then this crazy guy jumps out at her and almost murders her but she escapes by jumping in the river and then she swims right into this bloated corpse and *then* when she staggers onto the bank there's this strange flickering light coming from the nearby graveyard and it's an evil occult sect wanting to sacrifice an innocent young girl and she's *just* what they're looking for . . .

Tracy thinks she's written a masterpiece but her teacher, Mrs Bagley, isn't particularly appreciative. She tells Tracy she has a very warped imagination. I'm sure my Mr Townsend would have encouraged Tracy! It's tough that she has Mrs Vomit Bagley for *her* teacher. They are *never* going to see eye to eye.

27

Mr Branson

Mr Branson took the top Juniors. We nicknamed him Brandy Balls. We weren't being particularly rude. Brandy Balls were reddish aniseed sweets, very popular in the 1950s. Even so, no child ever called Mr Branson Brandy Balls to his face. We didn't even call him Mr Branson. He was *Sir*, and we stood up when he came into the room, we stood up when he spoke to us, we stood up when we needed to speak to him, we stood up and stayed standing up, hands on head, if we'd been disobedient.

He wasn't a dear gentle friend to us like Mr Townsend. He was a teacher. I can't remember him caning any of the boys but we were all frequently terrified of him. He had a habit of whacking you across the knuckles with a ruler if he felt you needed to get a move on with your writing. If you settled into a little daydream, he'd aim his sharpened chalk at you with surprising accuracy, so that it really stung. If you were ever unwise enough to yawn, you had to run round the playground five times to get some oxygen into your lungs. He urged you to go 'Faster! *Faster!*' until your lungs weren't just freshly oxygenated, they were in danger of total collapse.

We might not have called him nicknames to his face but he had plenty for us, mostly unpleasant. I managed to be Top Girl some of the time, in spite of my lamentable maths, so I think he quite liked me. In fond moods he'd call me Jacky Daydream, almost a term of endearment for Mr Branson. He could also be cruel though. He frequently called me Four Eyes, a nickname I hated, as I was very self-conscious about wearing my new glasses. He also called me Sly Boots because when he stood over me in class, I was so intimidated I didn't dare look up at him.

'You're sly, Jacky, that's what it is. I can't stand people who won't look me in the eye.'

I did my best to meet his fierce bloodshot gaze, my eyelids twitching behind my awful fancy glasses.

I got off easily. He was particularly hateful to the slow and the stuttering, proclaiming them morons and imitating their stammer. He was worst of all to Julian, the most intelligent boy in the class – no, the whole *school*, including the teachers. Mr Townsend had encouraged Julian to ask questions. Mr Branson sighed heavily whenever Julian waved his hand. He'd imitate Julian's voice and encourage the rest of us to laugh at him. He'd call Julian Brainy Bonce or the Professor or His Lordship. Julian continued valiantly waving his hand in class no matter how many times Mr Branson belittled him.

He was unspeakably unkind – and yet he was a brilliant teacher, particularly in English. He was very keen on extending our vocabulary. He'd hand out tattered orange textbooks every week in a special vocabulary lesson. There would be twenty questions and we had to guess the twenty esoteric, extraordinary words on the blackboard in his neat teacher's writing. Then came the best part of the lesson. He'd make up a story incorporating all twenty words, always a bizarre, funny fantasy story that had us laughing our heads off – and effortlessly remembering the definition of every single word.

Mr Branson encouraged us to tell stories too. He asked what we'd been reading and got us to recount the plot. He often picked me to say what I was currently reading, though he pooh-poohed my girly choices. One day I told him I'd been reading *The Prince and the Pauper*. He looked surprised, even impressed. This definitely wasn't a girly book. It was a long, hard, difficult book by Mark Twain. I hadn't actually read the *book*. I'd read a comic-strip version, a Children's Illustrated Classic, luridly coloured and simplified. Still, it gave me a grasp of the story, so I started telling it at great length, embellishing as I went. The bell for play time went long before I was done.

'We'll have the rest after play time,' said Mr Branson.

So after the break I went and stood in front of the class again.

'*The Prince and the Pauper* – part two!' I said.

They all laughed, but seemed keen for me to continue.

The best lesson of all was the last lesson on Friday afternoons. Mr Branson would read aloud to us. He scorned Namby-Pamby Blyton and all her contemporaries. Mr Branson read us boys' tales of derring-do, late-Victorian adventure stories. I usually hated that sort of story, but Mr Branson was so brilliant at reading aloud that the boys in the book ran through our classroom, seizing our hands and whirling us away with them. We climbed mountains, we jumped across ice floes, we swung on creepers through the jungle. When the bell went for the end of afternoon lessons, our heads jerked with the shock of shooting back to the stuffy classroom. We all *groaned* because it was going-home time!

Mr Branson had high expectations of us. He prepared us with regimental precision for our eleven plus exam. There were two non-fee-paying grammar schools in Kingston – Tiffins Boys and Tiffins Girls – but the catchment area was huge and it was very difficult to pass highly enough to get a place. Mr Branson took pride in the fact that he prodded a handful of his class through the exam. If we failed, we were personally insulting him and his teaching ability. It made taking the eleven plus even more scary.

It loomed over us the moment we started in our top year. SATs tests are like little pimples compared with the huge boil of the 1950s eleven plus. None of us came from the sort of homes where private education was a possibility. The eleven plus was our one chance to get to a grammar school and stay on to do all the right exams and go into one of the professions. If you failed the eleven plus, you went to a secondary modern school and left at fifteen and started work straight away. You *worked* and therefore you stayed working class. Biddy and Harry and I hovered precariously between working class and lower middle class. Harry was a civil servant, we said 'lav' instead of 'toilet', we never dropped our aitches or said 'ain't'. I knew I had to live up to our aspirations.

Biddy didn't promise an incredible present if I passed the eleven plus. Most of my girlfriends had been promised a Pink Witch bike if they passed.

'I think that's just putting pressure on the poor kids,' Biddy said. 'I'd never do that to you, Jac. You just do your best, dear.'

She knew I'd try hard whether I was bribed or not. And I didn't want a Pink Witch bike. I couldn't ride *any* bike, pink or not.

Very few of the characters in my books ride bikes. I can only think of one girl. Who is it, and which book does she appear in?

It's Treasure in my book *Secrets*.

There was a girl cycling round and round too, doing fantastic wheelie tricks on a BMX. She looked every bit as tough as the boys, her hair tousled, a big red scar on her forehead, her face pale and pinched. She was so skinny in her tight jeans and tiny matted fleece. I stared at her enviously.

She saw me staring. She stuck her tongue out at me.

I waggled mine back at her.

Then she grinned. I grinned. It was just as if we knew each other.

I wanted to write about the friendship between two very different girls. Poor Treasure is going through a very tough time – but India isn't any happier, even though she lives in a big posh house and has any number of wonderful things. India is passionate about *The Diary of Anne Frank*. I read it when I was about India's age and thought it the most amazing, moving book too. I used to have a photo of Anne Frank on my bedside table.

498+355=

219+77=

66-24=

303+720=

432-91=

98+45=

1209+272=

28

The Eleven Plus

I had a filthy cold the day I took my eleven plus. One of those head-filled-with-fog colds, when you can't breathe, you can't hear, you can't taste, you certainly can't *think*. I was boiling hot and yet I kept shivering, especially when I was sitting there at my desk, ready to open the exam booklet. I knew I wouldn't have a hope in hell with the arithmetic part. I felt as if those eight mythical men were digging a hole in my head, shoving their spades up my nostrils, tunnelling under my eyes, shovelling in my ears.

I knew copying was out of the question. I wouldn't just risk the wrath and sorrow of Marion and her best friend, Jesus. We'd all been told very sternly indeed that anyone caught copying would be drummed out of the exam, the school, the town of Kingston, England, the World, the entire Universe – left to flounder in Space, with every passing alien pointing their three green fingers and hissing, '*Cheat!*'

'Open your paper and begin!' said Mr Branson. 'And read the questions *properly*.'

I read the questions. I re-read the questions. I read them till my eyes blurred. Pens were scratching all around me. I'd never felt so frightened in my life. I didn't know the answer to a single problem. I could do the simple adding up and taking away at the beginning. Well, I thought I could. When I picked up my pen at last and tried to write in my first few answers, the figures started wriggling around on the page, doing little whirring dances, and wouldn't keep still long enough for me to count them up. I couldn't calculate in my bunged-up head. I had to use my ten fingers, like an infant. I *felt* like an infant. I badly wanted to suck my thumb and rub my hankie over my sore nose, but if Mr Branson saw me sucking my thumb, he'd surely snip it off with his scissors like the long-legged Scissor Man in *Struwwelpeter*. I did try to have a quick nuzzle into my hankie, but it was soggy and disgusting with constant nose-blowing, no use at all.

I could manage the English, just about, but the intelligence test was almost as impenetrable as the arithmetic. The word games were fine, but the number sequences were meaningless and I couldn't cope with any questions starting: *A is to B as C is to?* Indeed! What did they mean? What did *any* of it mean?

I struggled on, snuffling and sighing, until at long last Mr Branson announced, 'Time's up! Put your pens *down*.'

My pen was slippy with sweat. I blew my nose over

and over again while everyone babbled around me.

'It was OK, wasn't it?' said my new friend Christine.

'It wasn't *too* bad,' said Marion.

'I liked that poem in the English part,' said Ann.

'My pen went all blotchy – do you think it matters?' said Cherry.

The boys were all boasting that it was easy-peasy, except Julian, who modestly kept quiet.

I kept quiet too.

'How did *you* get on, Jacky?'

'I thought it was horrible,' I sniffed.

'Oh, rubbish. You're one of the cleverest. I bet you'll come out top,' said Cherry.

'No I won't! I couldn't do half of the arithmetic,' I said.

'Neither could I,' said Christine comfortingly. 'But you'll have done all right, just you wait and see.'

Well, I waited. We all had to wait months until the results came through. Then Mr Branson stood at the front of the class with the large dreaded envelope. He opened it up with elaborate ceremony and then scanned it quickly. We sat up straight, hearts thumping. He took our class register and went down the long list of our names, ticking several. Every so often his hand hovered in the air and he made his mouth an O, hissing with horror.

He had the register at such an angle that we had no way of knowing whether he was up in the As or down in the Ws. We just had to sit there, sweating.

Mr Branson cleared his throat.

'Well, well, well,' he said. 'A lot of shocks and surprises here. Well done, *some* of you. The rest of you should be thoroughly ashamed. Very well, Four A, pin back your ears. I will now go through the register and tell you whether you have – or have not – passed your eleven-plus examination.'

He paused. We waited. I was Jacqueline Aitken then, the first child on the register.

'Jacky Aitken . . . you have *not* passed your eleven plus,' said Mr Branson.

I sat still, the edge of the desk pressing into my chest. Mr Branson glared at me, and then worked his way down the register. I couldn't concentrate. I heard Robert had passed, Raymond had passed, Julian of course had passed – but I didn't catch any of the girls' names. I was too concerned with my own terrible failure.

I wanted to cry, but there was no way in the world I was going to let Mr Branson see me weeping. I even managed to meet his eye.

I could face up to him but I didn't know how I was going to face Biddy and Harry. Biddy had said all the right things. She had tried not to put too much pressure on me. She'd told me simply to do my best. But I hadn't done my best, I'd done my worst. I'd failed. *She* hadn't failed. She'd passed her eleven plus and gone to Tiffins Girls.

Harry had been sent to a technical school so he was particularly keen for me to have a grammar school education. He'd tried tutoring me at home, working our way through intelligence tests and those terrible men-digging-holes problems. He'd start with his kind voice and he'd promise he wouldn't get cross. He said if there was anything at all I didn't understand, I had only to say and he'd go over it again for me. He'd go over it – again and again and again – and I'd struggle to take it all in, but the words started to lose all their sense and the figures were meaningless marks on the page.

'You're not *listening*, Jac!' Harry would say.

'I am. I am. You said you wouldn't get cross.'

'I'm *not* cross,' Harry insisted, sighing irritably.

He'd say it all again, s-l-o-w-l-y, as if that would somehow make a difference. I'd be just as baffled, and make silly mistakes, until Harry would suddenly lose it.

'*Are you a MORON?*' he'd shriek, his fist thumping the page.

I felt I *was* a moron where maths was concerned, but no one seemed to understand that I wasn't one *deliberately*. Harry spent hours and hours trying

289

to coach me even though it had now proved a total waste of time.

I had to tell them as soon as possible to get it over with. I couldn't ring them. Mobiles weren't invented. We didn't even have an ordinary land line at home. Harry possibly had one in the London office but I didn't know the number. I didn't know Biddy's number either, but I knew where her office was. I decided to miss my school dinner and run the two miles to her work to tell her the terrible news.

Poor Biddy. There she was, having a cup of tea and writing beautiful entries in the big accounts book when I burst in on her. Her pen wavered, her tea spilled, but she didn't care. She thought I'd passed. Surely that was the only reason I'd run such a long way at dinner time.

'Oh, Jac!' she said, holding out her arms, her whole face lit up with joy at the thought of her daughter going to grammar school.

'No, no – I've *failed*!'

She was valiant. She kept right on smiling and gave me the hug.

'Never mind,' she said. 'Never you mind. There now.' She paused. 'Did you get given a second chance?'

In those days they let all borderline eleven plus failures sit a further exam in the summer, and those who passed had their pick of the secondary schools. You couldn't get into Tiffins, but it still wasn't to be sniffed at.

I'd been in such a state I hadn't taken it in. I *had* been given a second chance. I went along to sit the exam a couple of months later. Ironically, we were all sent to Tiffins to do the paper. It was more scary not being in our own environment. No one told us where the lavatories were, so we all fidgeted desperately in our seats as time went by. I can't remember any men digging holes this time. Perhaps we only had to do an intelligence test. Anyway – this time I passed.

The twins in Double Act *sit an entrance exam to go to the boarding school Marnock Heights. Which twin passes, Ruby or Garnet?*

It's Garnet – although everyone expected Ruby to pass.

We couldn't believe it. We thought Miss Jeffreys had got us mixed up.

'She means me,' said Ruby. 'She must mean me.'

'Yes, it can't be me,' I said. 'Ruby will have got the scholarship.'

'No,' said Dad. 'It's definitely Garnet.'

'Let me see the letter!' Ruby demanded.

Dad didn't want either of us to see it.

'It's addressed to me,' he said. 'And it's plain what it says. There's no mix-up.'

'She's just got our names round the wrong way,' Ruby insisted. 'It's always happening.'

'Not this time,' said Rose.

'Look, it's absolutely not fair if she's read the letter too, when it's got nothing to do with her. She's not our mother,' said Ruby.

'No, but I'm your father, and I want you to calm down, Ruby, and we'll talk all this over carefully.'

'Not till you show me the letter!'

'I'd show both the girls the letter,' said Rose. 'They're not little kids. I think they should see what it says.'

So Dad showed us.

It was like a smack in the face.

Not for me. For Ruby.

Poor Ruby – and poor Garnet too! I hate the next bit, when Ruby refuses to have anything to do with Garnet. I'm glad they make friends again just before Garnet goes off to boarding school. I've often wondered what happens next!

29

Fat Pat

I still had imaginary friends when I was in the last year of Latchmere but I had many real friends too. I still walked to and from school with Cherry but I didn't play with her so much. I didn't play with Ann any more either. She had a new best friend, a tall rangy girl called Glynis. They were always going off together and playing their own elaborate secret games. Ann was prettier than ever, her hair long and glossy and tied with bright satin bows. She wore wonderful short floral dresses with smocking and frilled sleeves. She had frills all over – when she ran, you caught a glimpse of her white frilly knickers. She was the girl we all wanted to be.

Poor Pat was the girl we all shunned. She was the fat girl, Fat Pat, Chubby Cheeks, Lardy Mardy, Greedy Guts, Two-Ton Tessie, Elephant Bum. She wore sensible loose dresses to hide her bulk. It must have been torture for her to have to take off her dress publicly and do PT in her vest and vast knickers. If she'd been half her size she'd have been considered pretty. She had very pink cheeks and long blonde straight hair, almost white. Her plaits were always incredibly neat, never a hair out of place, her ribbons tied up all day long.

She had the most beautifully neat handwriting too. She'd lie half across her page, her chubby hand moving slowly, her pink tongue peeping out between her lips – so much effort to make those smooth, even, blue letters on the page.

I don't think she had any friends. She wasn't particularly teased in the playground. She was simply shunned.

I shunned her too in front of the others, but if we happened to fetch up together – before school in the classroom, walking down the corridor, in the girls' toilets – I'd make a few hesitant overtures.

'I hope old Brandy Balls isn't in a bad mood today!'

'Can you work out how to do those problems? I haven't got a clue!'

'Hurray, it's raining! No PT! I do hope we can do country dancing instead.'

She'd smile at me and murmur something in reply. One day, when I found her combing the tails of her sleek plaits in the cloakroom, I said, 'You're so lucky to have such lovely long hair.'

I said it because I genuinely thought she had lovely hair. I was also trying to be kind, because Pat rarely got compliments. Her cheeks went a little pinker. She smiled at me and said nothing, but there was such a wry and wistful expression on her face. She knew why I was saying it. She felt pleased but patronized. Why should she feel humbly grateful for a crumb of kindness? Why should she be singled out to be the sad girl in the class? She didn't seem to eat more than anyone else. She wasn't lazy. She puffed along heroically after us when we were made to run round and round the playground.

'I can't *help* being fat,' she said. 'It's my metabolism.'

I didn't know what her metabolism was. I imagined it like a night monster, crouching on her chest in the small hours, funnelling double cream and melted chocolate up her nostrils as she slept.

I nodded sympathetically. 'It doesn't matter, being fat,' I said, though we both knew it mattered tremendously.

Pat wasn't taken seriously by anyone at school. She wasn't allowed to be Pat the Person, with her own personality. She was simply Fat Pat, a sad cartoon girl waddling in our midst.

Then she suddenly wasn't in our midst any more. We came back to school after a half-term holiday and she wasn't there. Her seat was empty. Her name wasn't called in register. We didn't really think anything of it. Not until we filed into assembly and saw Mr Pearson standing on the stage, looking very grave.

'I've got some very sad news for you, children. I'm sure you all know Pat in Mr Branson's class. I'm afraid she passed away during the holiday. Our thoughts are with her poor parents. Let us all say a prayer for Pat.'

I shut my eyes and bent my head, utterly stunned. I hadn't really known anyone before who had *died*. Harry's mother had died when I was a baby, Harry's father had died when I was a small child, but they were old to me. Pat was *my* age. She was poor Fat Pat, the girl I chatted to in the toilets, the girl I shamefully ignored in the classroom. But now she'd done something as extraordinary and dramatic and grown up as dying.

I thought of her squashed into a white coffin, her plaits tied with white satin, dressed in a long white nightie. I wondered if her cheeks would still be pink. I thought of her lying in her coffin week after week after week, getting thinner and thinner and thinner until she dieted down to a skeleton. I started to shake. I wished I'd been kinder to her. I wished I'd been her friend all the time. I hadn't properly *known* her so I couldn't really miss her, but it felt as if I did.

I don't think anyone told us what she died *of*. I have a vague feeling it might have been an asthma attack, but I don't remember her ever using an inhaler. Maybe children didn't have them in those days.

We didn't talk about Pat amongst ourselves. I think we all felt guilty. We tried to forget her, but she's there in our form photograph, smiling bravely, as if she was just an ordinary happy-go-lucky member of our class. And now, when I look at that faded black and white photo, I realize she wasn't even *that* fat. I don't need to look at the photo to remember her. I often think about her even now.

> *I have a very cheery, confident fat boy in three of my books. What is his nickname – and can you think of all three titles?*

It's Biscuits, and he appears in *Cliffhanger*, *Buried Alive* and *Best Friends*.

I suppose I'm still a bit greedy, if I'm absolutely honest. Not quite as greedy as Biscuits though. Well, his real name is Billy McVitie, but everyone calls him Biscuits, even the teachers. He's this boy in our class at school and his appetite is astonishing. He can eat an entire packet of chocolate Hob Nobs, munch crunch, munch crunch, in two minutes flat.

Biscuits is so kind and funny and positive – and a *marvellous* friend. He's very supportive of Tim when they're on their adventure holiday in *Cliffhanger*, and they have even more fun on a seaside holiday in *Buried Alive*.

I decided I wanted to find out more about dear old Biscuits, so he popped up again in *Best Friends*.

Gemma gives him a hard time, but *eventually* appreciates him. Biscuits makes brilliant cakes, including a wonderful chocolate biscuit cake. One Christmas my lovely friend and illustrator Nick Sharratt made *me* a fantastic chocolate biscuit cake, very rich and munchy, studded with red glacé cherries. My mouth's watering remembering it!

Ann   Marion   Christine

30

Christine

I made a new friend in Mr Branson's class. She was called Christine, a tall girl with a high forehead and glossy brown hair cut short and clipped back with tortoiseshell hairslides. She went glossy brown all over every summer, effortlessly and evenly tanning, while I went red and blotchy and then peeled.

Christine was six months older than me. She'd been in the class above but now she'd been kept back to repeat a year. She was bright as a button but there were problems at home. I don't think Christine had even sat the eleven plus last year. She couldn't move on to a secondary school because they were all too far away. Christine needed to dash home every lunch time to see her mother.

'My mum's dying,' Christine told me, as soon as we'd made friends.

We huddled up together in the playground, arms round each other, while she told me all about it. Christine told it straight, no soft euphemisms, though the teachers murmured about her mother being 'poorly'.

'She's got cancer,' said Christine. 'She's had it for ages and now it's so bad she can't do anything. She just lies on the sofa downstairs. She's got so thin and she looks so old, not really like my mum any more. But she's still my mum inside, even though she gets muddled and sleepy with all the drugs she has to take.'

'The drugs?' I whispered.

'For the pain. She gets in such awful pain,' said Christine. She said it matter-of-factly, but her eyes watered. 'I give her her dose at lunch time and I take her to the toilet and fix her a drink. She sleeps a bit then, but the drugs wear off. She's often crying by the time I get home. It's the worst pain ever.'

I tried to think what the worst pain ever must be like. I thought of all my tummy upsets, when I sometimes doubled up involuntarily. I imagined that much worse. I wondered how I would cope if it was my mum.

'Isn't there anyone else to help look after her?' I asked, taking Christine's hand.

'There's my dad, but he's out at work in London all day,' said Christine. (He was a civil servant and vaguely knew *my* dad.) 'Anyway, they don't really get on now. Daddy's got this girlfriend. But don't tell anyone.'

I nodded. This was something I understood.

'My mum's got a boyfriend. Don't tell either, OK?'

'I've got a big sister, but she keeps having heaps of rows with my dad and staying out late. She mostly stays round at her boyfriend's house. It's better when she does, it's more peaceful.'

'But it's not fair on you, having to do everything for your poor mum.'

'I don't mind. I *want* to do it. I want to help her,' said Christine.

'What about Patricia?' I said. 'Does she help too?'

She was Christine's sister in the year below, a fair, giggly girl, often acting a little wildly in the playground with her friend Madeleine, letting off steam.

'Patricia tries but she's not that good at making Mummy comfortable. And she gets too upset. She's just a baby,' said Christine, as if there was a lifetime between nine and eleven.

So Christine soldiered on, day after day, nursing her dying mother, doing most of the shopping, the washing, the ironing. She did this willingly, without complaint. The only thing she complained about bitterly was the fact that her mother was dying.

'It's not *fair*,' she said, clinging to me. 'She's so kind and gentle and lovely. Why should she have to die so young? I asked the vicar at our church and he said it's very sad but it's God's will. Well, I think God's a terrible person if he wants to make Mum suffer so much. I *hate* God.'

We stared at each other, both of us shocked at what she'd said. We waited for the thunderbolt to come sizzling out of the sky. Nothing happened.

'I don't blame you,' I said lamely. 'Oh, Christine, it isn't fair at all.'

I held her and rocked her. She cried a little and I cried too. Then we realized we were alone in the playground. Afternoon school had already started.

'Oh, lummy, I've made us late,' said Christine.

'Never mind.'

'Brandy Balls will go barmy.'

'Who cares,' I said, patting her.

We went into the classroom, holding our breath. Mr Branson was writing something on the blackboard. He stopped as we came in. He broke his chalk in two. He aimed one half at me, the other at Christine. He hit both of us on the temple where it hurt most.

'How *dare* you come into my classroom ten minutes late!' he thundered. 'What have you been doing, you idle lazy gossipy girls?'

I clenched my fists. 'I'll tell you what we've been doing!' I shouted back. 'Christine's been crying and I've been trying to comfort her. You *know* her mum's very ill. You know what Christine has to do. How *dare* you call her lazy and idle!'

The class sat statue-still, mouths open. They stared at me. Nobody ever ever ever answered Mr

Branson back. I'd obviously gone mental. They stared at Mr Branson, waiting for him to go to the cupboard and get out his cane. I waited too, trembling.

Mr Branson's face was purple. He stood still, making little snorty noises with his nose. A long blue vein throbbed on his forehead. Then he took a deep breath.

'Sit down,' he said.

I sat. Christine sat. Mr Branson took a new piece of chalk and continued writing on the board.

That was *it*! He carried on teaching and then left the classroom at the end of the lesson. I breathed out properly, almost collapsing. I couldn't believe it. I'd shouted at Mr Branson and survived! Perhaps he'd actually felt ashamed, realizing just how hard it was for Christine. But he didn't do anything to make it easier for her.

We didn't either. I was allowed to invite Christine for tea one Friday when her older sister was back at home. Christine and I shut ourselves in my bedroom and I showed her all my dolls, even my special secret paper girls. We got out all my art things and made ourselves cardboard badges with a C entwined with a J design, carefully coloured in Derwent crayon. We pinned our badges on solemnly with safety pins. We fingered all the beads in my shell box, holding the crystals to the light and marvelling at the rainbows. We lay on our tummies and drew portraits of each other.

Then we took a sheet of drawing paper and folded it up into squares to make a 'fortune-teller'. We sat cross-legged, deciding each other's fortune. We were so absorbed in our play we didn't want to stop for tea, so Biddy, with unusual tact, brought our meal in to us. We picnicked on banana sandwiches and cream buns and chocolate fingers and Tizer and then lolled against each other, flicking through old *Girl* comics.

Christine's father came to collect her very late, past my usual bed time. The adults chatted uncomfortably for a minute or so. The fathers exchanged pleasantries about work. Biddy said something about Christine's nice manners. Christine's mother wasn't even mentioned.

She died the day before we took our eleven plus. Christine came to school red-eyed but resolute. She sat the exam along with all of us – and passed.

Which character in my books has a mum who has cancer?

It's Lola Rose in the book of the same name.

Mum's fever went down, but she had to stay in hospital a while. Then she was well enough to come home, though she still had to go for her treatment. First the chemotherapy, weeks of it.

All Mum's beautiful long blonde hair started falling out after the second treatment. It was so scary at first. Kendall and I were cuddled up with her in bed in the morning and when she sat up great long locks of her hair stayed on her pillow.

'Oh my God,' Mum gasped. She put her hands to her head, feeling the bald patches. 'This is just like being in a bloody horror movie!'

I wanted to write truthfully about Victoria and her illness. She calls herself Lady Luck – and I do so hope she will be lucky and get completely better. She means so much to Lola Rose and her little brother Kendall. Still, they also have Auntie Barbara to look after them. I *love* Auntie Barbara. I wish I had one!

Jacky and Alan

31

Our Gang

Christine and I were best friends – but we were also part of a gang. There were our two boyfriends, David and Alan. They were best friends too. David was a freckle-faced, rather solemn boy with brown hair and clothes that my mother would call 'nobby'. David's mum had him wearing checked shirts and khaki shorts and baseball boots, clothes we'd consider cool now but were a little odd in the 1950s. Alan wore ordinary grey boy clothes. His sleeves were always rolled up, his collar open, his socks falling down, his sandals scuffed. He had straight fair hair, the sort that has to be smarmed down with water to stop it sticking straight up. He had a cheeky grin and a happy-go-lucky character.

David was my boyfriend; Alan was Christine's. It was all very convenient – though secretly I preferred Alan to David. One play time Christine talked a little wistfully about David.

'Do you really like him then?' I asked.

'Well, yes. As much as Alan. In fact more. But don't worry, Jacky, I know he's *your* boyfriend. I'd never ever try to take him off you.'

'Mm. Christine . . . the thing is, I like Alan. More than David. I wish we could swap.'

'Well . . . can't we?'

We tried to think of a tactful way of putting it to the boys. We didn't want to hurt their feelings. We didn't want them to go off in a huff and take up with two other girls.

'We *can't* tell them,' I said.

'Yes we can,' said Christine.

She was bossier than me and very determined. She caught my hand and pulled me over to the corner of the playground, where Alan and David were swapping cigarette cards with some other boys.

'Hey, Alan and David, Jacky and I want to talk to you,' she said.

They sighed and came over, shuffling their footballers and cricketers into separate packs.

Christine put her arms round their shoulders. 'We like you both very much, but Jacky was just wondering . . .'

'Christine!'

'OK, OK, *we* were wondering, how do you fancy swapping over for a bit? So you can be my boyfriend, David, and Alan, you can be Jacky's boyfriend.'

We waited, while David looked at Alan and Alan looked at David.

'Yep. That's fine,' said Alan.

'Fine with me too,' said David.

Then they went off to bargain for more cigarette cards and Christine and I went off to swap beads, all of us happy.

They weren't *proper* boyfriends, of course. We didn't go out with each other. I didn't go round to play at David's or Alan's and I wouldn't have dreamed of inviting them for one of Biddy's cream-bun teas. Our romances were very low key. We sometimes took turns giving each other 'a film-star kiss', but it was really just a quick peck. We wrote love letters to each other in class, but they were brief to the point of terseness, though for years I treasured a crumpled piece of paper saying, 'Dear Jacky, I love you from Alan.' I was far closer to Christine, to Ann, to Cherry – and to another new friend Eileen.

She wasn't a new girl but she *seemed* new in Mr Branson's class. She'd been away from school for a couple of months in Mr Townsend's class with a badly broken leg. I remembered her as a curly-haired pixie-faced girl, maybe a little babyish for her age. She came into Mr Branson's class transformed. She'd grown several inches. Not just upwards. She had a chest!

She was the first girl in our class to wear a real bra. The boys teased her as soon as they found out and twanged her bra at the back, but Eileen managed to slap them away and keep them in their place. She looked so much older than everyone that she had sudden authority. She swished around the playground in her full patterned skirts, her small waist cinched in with an elasticated belt. She had an air of mystery about her, as if she knew all sorts of secrets. Well, she did. She sat in a corner with Christine and me and told us what it was like to have a period. We knew some of this Facts of Life stuff already, but it was interesting to have Eileen telling us practical details.

We must have been a satisfying audience, Christine and I, with our short haircuts and little white socks and Clarks sandals. Eileen elaborated, telling us things that seemed utterly unlikely – and yet maybe people *really* did this or that? She also told us about some sort of boyfriend she'd met in the summer holidays, Mr Honey. I *hope* he was complete fantasy.

Eileen had a real boyfriend at school now, red-haired Robert, a small, eager boy almost as bright as Julian. Robert seemed an unlikely match for this new sexy Eileen in his short trousers and pullovers and black plimsolls, but they seemed a happy couple for all that. Julian came to play with us too, though he didn't have a girlfriend himself. So this was our gang – Christine, David, Alan, Eileen, Robert, Julian and me.

We started to play together every day. We had our own special club and a badge, and we had to use particular green biros whenever we wrote to each other. We called ourselves the Secret Seven, like the Enid Blyton books, but now we had Eileen with us we didn't act like Blyton children.

Mr Branson always chivied us when he was on playground duty. We liked to sit huddled together against the wall of the boys' toilets – not, I suppose, the most attractive location. Mr Branson would kick the soles of our feet in irritation.

'Come on, you lot, stop flopping there like a bunch of rag dolls. Go and have a run round the playground, get some fresh air into your lungs.'

He'd harangue us until we got up, groaning, and jog-trotted round and round. It wasn't just Mr Branson who picked on us. All the teachers started trying to get us to separate, even our dear Mr Townsend, suggesting skipping for Christine and Eileen and me, football for the boys. We were puzzled at first. Christine and Eileen and I loathed skipping, and felt we were too old to jump up and down chanting:

> *'Nebuchadnezzar, King of the Jews,*
> *Bought his wife a pair of shoes.*
> *When the shoes began to wear,*
> *Nebuchadnezzar began to swear.*
> *When the swear began to stop,*
> *Nebuchadnezzar bought a shop.*

When the shop began to sell,
Nebuchadnezzar bought a bell.
When the bell began to ring,
Nebuchadnezzar began to sing,
Do ray me fah so la ti dooooooo!

You had to whirl the skipping rope twice as fast for the last part, doing 'bumps' until you tripped. I always tripped as soon as I started bumping because my arms wouldn't whirl round fast enough, but who cared anyway?

The boys were even less keen on football. They were gentle, dreamy boys who didn't want to charge round shouting and kicking. Mr Townsend *knew* this. Why did he suddenly want to break us up and make us start being sporty?

I think the teachers were scared we were growing up too soon. Maybe all this boyfriend/ girlfriend stuff alarmed them, though it was all perfectly innocent. Eileen probably unnerved them, with her knowing look and new figure.

We took to huddling right at the very edge of the playground, behind the canteen, hoping that none of the teachers would spot us there, but if *they* didn't find us, some bossy form monitor would creep round the corner and pounce on us.

Then *I* was made a very special monitor – and all our problems were solved.

*In one of my books there's a girl who talks
with a fake American accent and acts
much older than she really is.
Do you know which book it is?*

It's *Candyfloss.*

'Open your present, Floss. You're such a slowpoke,' said Margot.

She meant *slowcoach*. She's got this irritating habit of talking in a fake American accent and using silly American expressions. She thinks it makes her sound sophisticated but I think she sounds plain stupid.

I could make a l-o-n-g list of reasons why I can't stick Margot. She used to be ordinary – in fact I can barely remember her back in the baby classes – but *this* year she's making out she's all grown up. She's always giggling about boys and sex and pop stars. Judy giggles too. She looks as babyish as me but she's got an older brother who tells her all these really rude jokes. I don't understand most of them. I'm not sure Judy does either.

Floss doesn't like Margot because she's very worried her friend Rhiannon will go off with her.

But by the end of *Candyfloss* Floss has found a
much nicer friend.

Christine Alan Robert Eileen David Julian

32

The Secret!

I wasn't made a form monitor. I was always too dreamy and likely to do something silly. I *certainly* wasn't games monitor material. I was never one of the ultra-helpful children made flower monitor or milk monitor. But Mr Branson had a soft spot for little Jacky Daydream/Four Eyes/Sly Boots, even though I'd dared yell at him in class. On the first of December he made me Christmas card monitor.

Our year was the top year, head of the Juniors, so we had various responsibilities. Every Christmas term a shiny scarlet postbox stood in the entrance hall. All the Juniors posted their Christmas cards into its wide slot. It was a big postbox, carefully constructed out of thick cardboard and given a new coat of paint every few years, but it wasn't big enough to contain everyone's cards. It was my job as Christmas card monitor to bustle along every morning, unlatch the little brass hinges so that the door at the back swung open, and then empty out all yesterday's letters.

The head teacher himself, Mr Pearson, showed

me where I had to sort and store the letters. There were two doors next to his room. I was familiar with the first door. It lead into a dark storeroom where we kept the sacks of milk-bottle tops, saved and recycled. No one washed the tops so the room reeked of sour milk. I hated any kind of milk, even fresh from the cow. If I was ever sent to the storeroom, I held my cardie sleeve over my nose and tried not to breathe in. I wasn't sure I was going to be able to stand being Christmas card monitor if I had to sort them while being gassed by sour milk fumes.

But Mr Pearson was opening the other door. This was my fourth year in the Juniors and I must have seen that door every day, yet I had no idea what was behind it. It was another storeroom, full of trunks and old desks and blackboards and easels. Mr Pearson patted the biggest flat-topped trunk.

'Here you are, Jacky, you can sort the cards into forms on this top. Stack them all neatly now. And then on the last day of term you can come with me when I dress up as Santa Claus and you can be my special Christmas elf delivering all the cards,' he said.

I smiled gratefully, though I didn't exactly go a bundle on being an *elf*. I prayed I wouldn't have to wear a silly costume or false pointy ears.

I went along to collect the posted cards the

322

second morning. There were only a handful, but I took them out carefully, with due ceremony, opened up the storeroom door and started sorting them in sparse piles on top of the trunk. It only took a minute or so. I ran my finger along the brass studs of the trunk. I wondered what was inside. I collected the cards back into a pile, picked them up and then tried edging the lid open. It didn't budge at first so I thought it must be locked, but when I had one more try with two hands, the lid creaked and then jerked upwards. I lifted it right up and stared awestruck at the contents of the trunk.

Treasure! Gold crowns, silver chains, necklaces, rings, crystal goblets, an entire gold tea-set! I'd read all my Enid Blyton adventure books. What *else* would you expect to find in an old trunk but buried treasure?

It wasn't *real*. The jewels were Rowntrees Fruit Gums, the gold was paint, the silver chocolate wrappers. These were the props from past school plays. I recognized the Three Wise Kings' crowns, the banquet christening plates from *The Sleeping Beauty*. I dug a little deeper. My fingers touched fur, slippery silk, soft velvet. It was all the costumes!

I carefully piled all the fake jewellery and cardboard china onto the floor and pulled out robes and capes and ballgowns galore. I held them up against me, wishing there was a mirror. I found a beautiful long crinoline made of rich purple velvet. I slipped it over my head and then twirled round and round, bumping into boxes in the crowded room.

I played being a Victorian lady, festooning myself with jewellery and giving imperious orders to invisible servants – but for once it wasn't enough to pretend by myself. This find was too marvellous to keep a total secret. I had to share it with Christine.

Back in Mr Branson's class I hooked her silky hair back behind her ear and whispered what I'd found. She looked sceptical at first. She knew my habit of romancing.

'Are you sure you're not making it up, Jacky?'

'You come and see too, tomorrow!'

So Christine hovered behind me the next morning while I undid the letter box and clawed out all the Christmas cards. We waited until the hallway was empty – no teachers, no crying children who'd fallen over in the playground, no mothers waiting to speak to Mr Pearson, and definitely *no* Mr Pearson himself. Then I opened the storeroom door and we scuttled inside.

'See!' I said, lifting the lid of the trunk.

'Oh glory!' said Christine, fingering the crowns, the necklaces, the purple velvet crinoline. 'Oh, Jacky, it's fantastic! This is the best secret *ever*!'

I let her try on the purple velvet dress. I

struggled into a crimson tunic and an ermine-lined cape. I bowed low before her.

'Might I have the honour of a dance, fair Lady Christine?'

'Certainly, my Lord Jack,' said Christine.

We were neither of us quite sure how you did stately dancing, but we twirled a bit and did a lot more bowing and curtseying. Christine climbed up on a chest to pose in a regal fashion, waving a fairy wand. Then she twitched it at the darkest corner, behind a blackboard.

'There's a door at the back, look!'

We clambered over the boxes and chests to get to it. I put my hand on the doorknob, hesitating.

'Maybe it's Mr Pearson's secret room. Perhaps he's in there, cuddled up with Miss Audric!'

We snorted with laughter, clutching each other.

'Open it, go on,' said Christine.

I turned the handle and the door opened. We could dimly see stairs going upwards.

'A secret passage!' said Christine. 'Come on, let's see where it goes.'

Hand in hand, we tiptoed up and up the dark staircase, barely able to catch our breath with the excitement. There was yet another door at the top. We opened it and stepped out into sudden bright daylight. We stood blinking, disorientated, staring at the wooden rail in front of us. There was the hall stage before us, with the school piano – but we were standing way above it now.

'We're up in the gallery!' I said.

I suppose we should have realized sooner, but the gallery was very seldom used. The choir sang there for special concerts, but that was all. We never looked at the gallery because we always faced the stage as we filed in for assembly. But now we were actually up in the gallery, so high we could almost touch the ceiling. It felt as if we'd grown wings and flown there.

Then we heard the clacking of stout heels down below on the parquet floor. We saw Miss Audric's red plaits and her emerald-green woollen suit. We both had a vision of her curled on Mr Pearson's lap like a giant woolly caterpillar. We clamped our hands over our mouths to stifle our giggles.

Miss Audric hitched up her long wool skirt, climbed the steps to the stage and sat at the piano. She waggled her fingers several times as if she was waving at the keys and then she started playing Handel's *Water Music*, ready for us to start coming into the hall for assembly.

'Quick!' I said.

We crept backwards to the door, lifting our feet so our rubber-soled sandals wouldn't squeak on the wooden floor. Then we shot through the door and tumbled down the stairs, laughing wildly, clutching each other.

We slipped inside the storeroom every morning and played dressing up. It was hard coping with such a splendid secret. It fizzed inside us all the time until we felt ready to explode.

'What's *up* with you two?' said Eileen.

'Yes, where do you and Christine keep hiding, Jacky?' said Alan.

'Yeah, you keep sneaking off somewhere before school,' said David.

'Have you found a special secret place?' asked Julian.

'Tell us!' said Robert.

Christine and I looked at each other. We *had* to tell them.

They were desperate to see for themselves but it was too difficult to sneak them all in before school. Besides, everyone arrived at different times, and Eileen and David were often late.

I thought about lunch time. It was quieter in the school entrance then. There was always the risk of running into Mr Pearson – but at twelve thirty the school cook brought him his lunch on a tray and he ate his meal in private in his room.

'OK, here's the plan,' I said. 'We wait five minutes after the bell goes, and then at twelve thirty-five we creep into the school entrance. Mr Pearson will be in his study tucking into his lunch, so he won't be doing any prowling about. But we'll

327

have to be as quiet as mice.'

Julian started squeaking and scuttling on all fours.

'And no messing about, OK! If Mr Pearson catches us, I shall be in *serious* trouble.'

Julian stood up quickly. They all blinked at me seriously. It was a heady moment being able to boss them all around, even Eileen.

They were as good as gold at lunch time. We waited in the playground, Robert checking his Timex watch every few seconds. Then Christine and Eileen and I went off together arm in arm. The boys followed in a little cluster, their cigarette cards splayed in their hands as if they were simply ambling off for a game of swapsies.

We crept into the school entrance, all of us staring fearfully at Mr Pearson's door. Then I took a deep breath, opened the door of the storeroom and shoved them all quickly inside – one, two, three, four, five, six, all seven of us, counting me.

The boys started squealing in triumph when we were all in.

'Ssh! We've got to be *quiet*! Mr Pearson's only just across the hallway!'

'Sorry, Jacky. Come on then, where are these costumes and all this other stuff?'

I swept the piles of Christmas cards out of the way – growing larger day by day – and opened the trunk. The boys weren't *quite* as impressed by the crowns and the jewellery but even they liked the costumes. Eileen adored everything. Christine and I offered her the purple velvet to be polite, but she preferred wrapping herself in long lengths of orange and scarlet and fuschia pink silk so that she glowed like an Indian princess. Robert found a pirate outfit with a patch, Alan was a sailor, David a policeman complete with helmet. Julian scooped up an enormous armful of fur. He stepped inside and became a large lollopy dog with floppy ears.

We played an imaginary game together as if we were still little kids in the Infants. It was as if the costumes liberated us from our real selves. We could be colourful fantasy creatures.

When the bell went for afternoon school, we had to whip all the costumes off quickly and then get out of the storeroom unobserved. Christine went first, taking David with her. Then Eileen and Robert. Then Julian and Alan. I waited a few seconds, looking round the storeroom, enjoying this moment of total happiness. Then I opened the door – and walked straight into Mr Pearson.

He peered at me over his spectacles. 'Jacky? What were you doing in the storeroom? You're only supposed to go in there when you're emptying the postbox.'

I saw Christine and the others standing agonized at the edge of the playground. We were all going to get into terrible trouble unless I kept my head.

I smiled at Mr Pearson. 'Yes, I know, Mr Pearson, but I was in a bit of a hurry this morning and I was scared of being late for Mr Branson so I didn't quite finish sorting yesterday's letters into classes. I thought I'd slip in at lunch time. I'm sorry.'

'That's quite all right, Jacky. I understand,' said Mr Pearson, smiling back at me.

There! I bet you were worried that we'd all be caught and punished, but we got away with it. We spent every lunch time playing in the storeroom until the end of term.

Many many years later I was invited to give a talk about my books at Latchmere. I had a cup of coffee and a chocolate biscuit beforehand in the head teacher's study. I was telling him all about my schooldays, and I mentioned the postbox.

'We still use it!' he said. 'Come with me.'

He took me into the storeroom and there was the red postbox in a corner – and the very same big trunk with the brass studs round the lid . . .

One of the characters in my books wears real Victorian clothes – but she doesn't have a beautiful purple crinoline. She has to wear uniform, stitched by herself. Who is it?

It's Lottie in *The Lottie Project*.

'Do you feel you can manage all this?' she said. 'You look very little.'

'But I am strong, Madam. I will manage,' I said determinedly.

'Very good. You can start on Monday. I will give you the print for your uniform and a bolt of cotton for your apron and caps. I hope you are satisfactory at sewing, Charlotte?'

I blinked at her. 'Charlotte, Madam?' I said foolishly.

'That is your name, it is not?' she said.

'No, Madam, I am called Lottie, Madam. It was the name of Mother's doll when she was small. No one's ever called me Charlotte.'

'Well, I do not think Lottie is a suitable name for a servant. You will be called Charlotte whilst you are working for me.'

I didn't need to do too much research about the Victorians when I was writing *The Lottie Project*. My daughter Emma loved everything Victorian and so I used to read her all sorts of old-fashioned stories. We had a huge 1880s Christmas catalogue and we spent happy hours choosing what we wanted! We also played special Victorian imaginary games. Emma always wanted to be the lady of the house, so I had to be the servant and curtsey to her and do everything she commanded. We wrote long rambling Victorian stories together too. Emma's were better than mine!

33

Bournemouth

The summer I left Latchmere we went on holiday to Bournemouth. We were branching out, staying in a three-star hotel for a whole fortnight.

I'd never been to Bournemouth before. It seemed to take for ever to get there. We still didn't have a car. We struggled with the suitcases on a Green Line bus from Kingston all the way up to London, lugged them down the escalators and onto the underground, and then onto the train to Bournemouth. We flopped down exhausted, and ate our egg sandwiches and Lyons fruit pies and Penguin chocolate biscuits, sharing a bottle of Tizer in plastic cups.

We branched out big-time when we finally arrived at Bournemouth railway station and got in a taxi. It was my very first taxi ride. Biddy and Harry sat bolt upright, their eyes on the meter. I slid around on the leather seat, worrying that there might be a terrible row if it proved too expensive. But it was a paltry sum, so Harry paid it willingly *and* gave the driver a tip.

We were all three impressed by Hinton Firs Hotel. It wasn't particularly *big*, just a perfectly normal family-size hotel, but it had that little extra touch of class. There was a welcome dance that first Saturday, so Biddy tweaked the flounces of her chiffon frock, Harry polished his patent shoes and I squeezed into my best C & A party frock with a sash and a lace collar.

There was no Will Tull urging us to be Music Men and join him in the conga, but there was a proper five-man band playing popular tunes in waltz and quickstep and foxtrot rhythms. There were little tables arranged around the edge of the dance floor so you could toy with a drink all evening. Alcohol! The holiday brochure hadn't mentioned the hotel was licensed! But Hinton Firs was ultra-respectable and we *were* on holiday. Biddy tried her very first Babycham and Harry had half a pint of lemonade shandy. I had orange squash, but Biddy let me have the maraschino cherry from her Babycham. I sucked it eagerly, hoping the drop of perry might make me drunk. Biddy and Harry sat stiffly among all these strangers, maybe hoping to feel drunk too.

Biddy got talking to the family at the next table who'd just arrived too – Mr and Mrs Hilton and their children, Diana and John. I wasn't remotely interested in John, a fair, fidgety boy of nine who pulled silly faces and strutted around with his hands in his pockets. I liked his sister Diana though. She was thirteen, a tall, curvy girl with a high forehead and blonde wavy hair. She wore pale pink lipstick, a blue dress cinched in at the waist, nylons and high heels. She looked years and years older than me. She already had the soft English rose looks that made men turn and stare at her. There weren't any other teenage girls staying in the hotel – so Diana made friends with me.

We chatted, sucking squash through straws, while our parents shuffled round the dance floor and John capered with the other boys in a corner. She told me all about her school and her friends at home and the boy she sometimes spoke to at her church youth club. I told her about Latchmere and Christine and said proudly that I had a boyfriend called Alan.

Then the band took a break to have a quick pint and someone started playing rock 'n' roll records – Tommy Steele and Bill Haley.

'Come on, Jacky, let's jive!' said Diana.

'I can't! I don't know how,' I said, blushing. 'I'll look silly.'

'No you won't,' said Diana. She nodded at John and the other boys, who were jerking around like crazy puppets. 'You certainly won't look as silly as *they* do.'

She took my hand and we got up to dance. She wasn't really an expert herself, tottering a little anxiously in her high heels, but she whirled me about, and once my feet caught the rhythm of the music, I started bouncing around, keeping to the beat, even improvising a few steps. I felt as if I could dance right across the ballroom, out of the window and up into the night, whirling round and round the clouds.

I was flushed and excited when I got back to our table, almost spilling my orange squash.

'Now, now, stop showing off,' said Biddy. 'Don't get above yourself, madam.'

But I *was* above myself, dancing and dancing with Diana, my new friend.

She had her very own single bedroom in the hotel, which impressed me enormously. John had to sleep on a put-you-up in her parents' room – and I still had to share with Biddy and Harry.

I tossed and turned that first night, too het up and excited to sleep properly. I was wide awake at six o'clock. I sat up stealthily in bed, reading *Wintle's Wonders* by Noel Streatfeild in the dawn light. I turned each page slowly and cautiously – but Harry suddenly started, turned over and opened his eyes.

I wriggled right down under the covers, hiding my book.

'Jac? What are you up to? Are you reading?'

I held my breath. For whatever crazy reason, I wasn't allowed to read if I woke up early. I was just supposed to lie there and try to get back to sleep. I was scared Harry would get cross with me. It would be terrible if he started a ranting fit right at the beginning of this beautiful Bournemouth holiday. But he leaned up on one elbow, actually smiling at me.

'It's OK. I can't sleep either. Shall we go for a walk before breakfast?'

'Oooh, yes!'

We took it in turns tiptoeing out of the bedroom to the lavatory and the bathroom. Hinton Firs was ultra posh to us but it didn't run to ensuite facilities. I pulled on my new blue jeans and checked shirt, hoping they might make me look like a real teenager, and hurried off with Harry.

We went along the quiet corridors, Harry shushing me, putting his finger to his lips. It was so strange thinking of all the sleeping guests the other side of each door, the men in their striped pyjamas, the women in artificial silk nighties, the children in white cotton patterned with teddies or tiny aeroplanes. We crept past Diana's small single room and I imagined her in a pink rosebud nightie, maybe a few curls pinned into place with kirby grips.

I wondered if she'd just been friendly at the dance because she had no one else to talk to, or whether she'd want to be my friend for the whole holiday. I imagined us walking along the sands, paddling in the sea, sharing secrets. Maybe she'd let me try her pink lipstick, stagger in her high sandals. I practised walking with precise steps, swaying my hips as we went down the stairs.

'Why are you walking in that daft way?' Harry whispered. It was all right, he wasn't cross, he seemed amused.

I shrugged. 'How old do you think I look, Daddy?' I asked.

'Oooh, twenty-two?'

'No, *really*.'

'Eleven.'

'Not maybe a bit older? I'll be twelve in December, and then it's only a year and then I'll be thirteen.'

'Your maths are improving,' Harry said dryly.

'I think I might almost look a teenager now,' I said, glancing at Harry for confirmation, but he only laughed at me.

Then we were outside the silent hotel in the fresh early morning air, the sun already out, the sky blue. There were tall pine trees and bright red and yellow flowers in every green garden. The hotels were white and pink and pale peach, one with brilliant blue roof tiles. I felt like Dorothy stepping into Oz.

'Oh glory, isn't it *lovely*!'

'Come on, let's see the sea,' said Harry, taking my hand. 'We haven't even caught a glimpse of it yet.'

340

We walked towards the front of East Cliff, swinging our clasped hands. Then I broke free and ran. The sea sparkled below me, intensely blue, incredibly beautiful. The sands shone smooth and golden for miles. There was a zigzag path cut into the side of the cliff, going right and left, right and left, all the way down to the esplanade below. I forgot all about wanting to act like a teenager. I ran full tilt down the zigzag path, arms high in the air, going, 'Wheeeee!'

When I got to the bottom, I stood panting, waiting for Harry to catch me up, and then I declared, 'I think Bournemouth is the most beautiful place in the whole world!'

It was certainly a beautiful holiday. For once my real life lived up to my imaginary one. I was usually slightly out of synch, like a children's comic when the colour is misaligned and the yellows and reds and blues bleed past the black outlines. But now I was jolted into place, the real world as colourful as anything I could imagine.

Biddy was up and dressed in her best white top with the embroidered poppies when we got back to our bedroom. She smiled at us with matching poppy-red lips.

'Have you had a nice walk, you two? Come on, I want my bacon and eggs for breakfast!'

The Hilton family were sitting at a big table

with three free spaces. Diana waved to me.

'Come and sit here, Jacky!'

We spent the whole holiday with them. Biddy and Harry and Mr and Mrs Hilton sat in deckchairs on the beach, while Diana and I went off together, John leaping around us boisterously, cracking daft jokes that made us sigh. We spent every day on the beach, swimming in the freezing sea and then jumping around, pale blue and shivering, until the sun dried us.

We made friends with a newly engaged couple, Bob and Shirley. Bob was a dark, good-looking rugby player in his twenties, ultra fit. Harry and Mr Hilton held in their soft stomachs when they were all in their bathing costumes. Diana and I developed a crush on this Bob and followed him around like puppy dogs. Shirley indulged us fondly, making a fuss of both of us. She lay back on his towel and smoothed suncream all over, turning golden brown, while Bob splashed in the sea with Diana and me and hurled John around like a human rugby ball.

I loved Diana, I loved Bob, I loved Shirley – I was so happy I even loved John. I loved Biddy and Harry, who even seemed to love each other this one magical holiday. They didn't have a single row the entire fortnight.

I woke up early every morning. Once, when both

my parents were still sleeping soundly, I pulled on my favourite jeans and shirt and slipped out of the room all by myself. I crept out of the hotel, through the garden, out of the gate, down the road, all the way to the clifftop. I stood gazing out at the turquoise sea, trying to find the right words in my head to describe it.

I wondered if I'd ever be a real writer. I'd finished *Wintle's Wonders* and was now reading my Puffin paperback of E. Nesbit's *Five Children and It*. I wondered what I would wish for if I encountered the irritable Psammead hiding in Bournemouth's golden sands.

'I wish, I wish, I wish,' I whispered, not knowing what to wish for. It was no use wishing that Biddy and Harry would stay happy together. I knew them too well to wish for that. It was a waste wishing to be a teenager, because I *would* be one soon. I could wish for Diana and me to stay proper friends after the holiday – but we'd already exchanged addresses, promising to write to each other. So I wished my usual wish, the one I wished when I blew out my birthday candles, when I spotted the first star of the evening, when I hooked the Christmas turkey wishbone round my little finger.

'I wish I get to be a real writer and have a book published one day.'

I wonder what I'd have thought if I could have

gazed over that brilliant blue Bournemouth sea far into the future. I wouldn't have believed it possible that one day I'd have *ninety* books published, not just one. I'd laugh at the idea that one amazing day children would queue up outside a bookshop in Bournemouth for eight whole hours simply so I could sign their books. *My* books!

I stared at the sea, the early sun already warm on my face.

'Bournemouth,' I said, tasting the word as if it was a boiled sweet.

Then I started running all the way down the zigzag path for the sheer joy of it, still wondering if wishes ever came true.

EPILOGUE
by Jacqueline Wilson

Whenever I give talks about my books children ask me all sorts of questions at the end. They ask me which is my favourite out of all my titles. I generally choose *The Illustrated Mum* because I tried particularly hard with that book and felt so sorry for poor little Dolphin. They ask how many books I've published and I say truthfully that I've lost count but over ninety now.

They ask how long it takes me to write a book and I ask them how long they think it takes. Sometimes the younger ones suggest it might take two or three days, or maybe a week, because that's how long it takes them to read one of my books. I so wish it really did just take a few days! It takes me at least six months to write a full-length book, and I'm actually a quick writer. I don't sit at my desk and write all day though – I'd find that incredibly boring and exhausting. I like to lead a busy and exciting life rushing round all over the place, going to bookshops and libraries and festivals to give talks, travelling to London to meet my agent and publishers, going to all sorts of committee meetings and charity events. I always take a notebook in my bag and when I'm in the back of a car or on a train I scribble away at the next bit of my story. It takes thirty minutes to travel on the train from Kingston to London. On a good day I can manage four or five hundred words by the time the train is drawing into Waterloo station. Then if I'm not too tired after my book-signing or meeting I can write another few hundred words on the way home. I get so lost in my imaginary world that I jump if someone sits next to me and says hello.

I spend a lot of time thinking about my story and wondering what's going to happen next. The moment my alarm goes off in the morning I have a little sleepy ponder about my book. Then I go for a swim and as I thrash backwards and forwards in the pool I'm still thinking about my characters and the twists and turns of the plot. Sometimes I get so absorbed I lose count of how many lengths I've done, which is annoying, because I like to do forty nowadays, and if I don't know the exact amount I feel I've cheated! I think about my novel on my way home, I make it up inside my head as I trudge round Sainsbury's and Marks and Spencer's, getting so absorbed that I frequently walk straight past friends without saying hello. I think about my story while I'm having lunch and supper, and always when I go to sleep so my characters drift in and out of my dreams.

Children often ask where I get my ideas from. I never quite know how to reply because I'm not really sure. I can't make an idea happen. I just have to keep my eyes open and my mind receptive. Sometimes I'm literally presented with my characters. I was on holiday in New York with my daughter Emma and we'd had a very busy day going round the Metropolitan

Museum and we'd also done a lot of shopping, so we needed to sit down somewhere. We went to Central Park and flopped on the grass, eating ice-creams. Central Park is always full of interesting people. We watched a very unusual arty looking young woman sauntering along. She had many intricate tattoos on her arms and legs, even on her neck. There were two tiny girls with her, in rather ragged dressing-up clothes, tottering in borrowed high-heeled sandals. When they were out of earshot Emma said to me, 'Don't they look like the sort of family you'd write about in one of your books!' I made a note about them there and then in my diary – and not long after, I started *The Illustrated Mum*.

Mostly though, I make up my characters from scratch, playing with them in my head the way I used to play with my dolls when I was little. Children don't always believe this though. The question I'm always asked is, 'Do you base your characters on yourself and your own personal experience?'

I've always said no, I make everything up. Think of all the very sad things that happen to all the girls in my books. If they'd actually all happened to me, I'd have had the most tragic childhood ever! I decided it might be a good idea to write my own story just to set the record straight. I knew right from the start I didn't want to write a memoir for adults. I write for children and so I wanted my autobiography to be for children too.

I started looking through the family photo album and trying to remember way back into the past. I began writing *Jacky Daydream*. It was a little strange at first writing about myself, and I had to be careful to stick to the true facts and not make anything up. I'm so used to storytelling that this was quite difficult! Still, I raced through the book and found it great fun to write.

When I'd finished I gave it to my daughter Emma to read. I wanted to make sure she approved. After all, I was writing the story of her family too. It was a great relief when she said she loved the book and didn't want me to change anything. I didn't show it to anyone else before sending it off to my publishers. Harry died long ago. Biddy is still very much alive – but I wasn't at all sure what she'd make of *Jacky Daydream*! She's never read any of my books so far, so I decided she probably didn't want to read this one either. I did tell her I was writing about my childhood but she didn't seem at all interested. However, when *Jacky Daydream* came out there was quite a lot of publicity about it, and several of my mum's friends read the book. When Biddy went in to her local over-sixties club one of these friends was there. 'Hello there, Biddy! We've been reading about you. Are you still seeing Uncle Ron?!' Biddy was outraged. She rang me up immediately and was very cross indeed. I don't suppose I blame her. I gave her a special copy of *Jacky Daydream* and she had a quick flick through but I don't think she's read it properly. Maybe it's just as well.

Biddy quite liked the family photographs being in the book. I prefer Nick's fantastic illustrations. I especially like the one of me in my best smocked dress pretending to be a ballet dancer. There's a copy of my favourite Noel Streatfeild book *Ballet Shoes* on the floor beside me. When *Jacky Daydream* came out, my lovely publishers took me for a very special meal at the Connaught Hotel in London. Emma came too and my best friend Trish, and Nick of course, and we all had a wonderful time. Annie, my editor, made a lovely speech and I said something too – and there were also presents, two fantastic books. Nick gave me a book about Old Cottage dolls because they were my very favourite dolls when I was young. My publishers gave me a beautiful first edition copy of *Ballet Shoes*!

It was a thrill when *Jacky Daydream* got great reviews and went to the top of the non-fiction books charts. I had so many letters about it. There were lots and lots from children. One little boy said that it was very interesting reading about 'olden times'! Many girls made lovely comments and said they identified with me because they loved reading and making up stories and playing imaginary games too.

I also got a surprising amount of letters from grown-ups. A lot of adults read the book because it reminded them of their own childhood and they wrote long moving letters telling me about their lives. I also got letters from people who used to know me long ago. The best letter of all was from dear Mr Townsend, my favourite teacher. I was so thrilled he'd read the book. I recognized his writing on the envelope, even after fifty years!

I have his writing on an old school report. I've just dug up all my old reports from Latchmere. I'll show them to you, thought they're not really interesting! They start when I'm in Form 2 – that's the equivalent of year 4. I was in lovely Mrs Simon's class, the lady who gamely dressed up as Father Christmas. There are two reports from her. I'm pleased that

---

LATCHMERE	
Report on: *Jacqueline Aitken*	Form: 2
Term Ending: *Summer 1955.*	

ENGLISH. Reading: *Excellent*

Spelling: *Very good*

Written Work: *Very fluent – imaginative*

ARITHMETIC. Mental: *Good*

Written: *Very good*

ART & Handwork: *Does well in this subject*

P.T. & Games: *Very good – keen and hard working*

- -

GENERAL:

Jacqueline is an excellent worker and has made good progress. – She is a pleasant pupil to teach. – Form 3 next term.

J. Pearson
Head.

K. Simon
Class Teacher.

---

she's complimentary about my writing, saying I show good written style and I'm very fluent and imaginative. But she also says my arithmetic is very good and gives me very good for

PT and games! Me, the child who couldn't add up for toffee and never once hit the ball in rounders. I think Mrs Simon must have given glowing reports on everyone. I ought to get nought out of ten for spelling now, because I see I've spelt her name wrong in chapter 25.

REPORT on **Jacqueline Aitken**, term ending July 23 '54
LATCHMERE C.P. JUNIOR SCHOOL.
Form: 2

ENGLISH. Reading: Very good
Spelling: Good
Written work: Shows good written style

ARITHMETIC: Mental. Fairly good
Written. Very good

ART & HANDWORK A neat & careful worker

P.T. and Games Very good — good team spirit.

GENERAL:

Jacqueline works very well. She is a sensible helper & always cheerful.

K. Simon.

LATCHMERE

	Form 3.	
Report on: J. Aitken.	EXAM.	MARKS OUT OF
Term Ending: 1956.		
ENGLISH Reading Very Good	9	10
Spelling: Good	17½	20
Written Work:		
Very Good	55	60
ARITHMETIC. Mental: Good	20½	25
Written:		
Very Good	58½	65
	160½	180
ART & Handwork:		
Good		
P.T. & Games:		
Average ability		
GENERAL : Jacqueline has worked		
very hard this year. She should do well		
in Form 4.		

[signature]   _L. R. Townsend._
Head.   Class Teacher.

I can only find one report from Mr Townsend. He gives me good marks and his comments are kind, if a little terse! He said I'd worked hard, which was true – I worked my socks off to impress him.

Then we come to Mr Branson's two reports on little Jacky Slyboots, Jacky Four Eyes, Jacky Daydream. They are astonishingly effusive! I can't even remember him ever praising me to my face, but here he is in the December report saying I'm an exemplary member of class in all ways!

LATCHMERE

Report on: Jacqueline Aitken   Form: 4

Term ending: Dec. 21st. 1956

English: Reading: 49/50

   Spelling: 21/25

   Written Work: 24/25 *Consistently*

   Formal work 37/50 *very good.*

   Composition 44/50

Arithmetic: Mental: 20/25

   written: 45/50 *Very good.*

   Speed 24/25

Art & Handwork: *Good*

P.T. & Games: *Good.* Exam. total 264/300

        Class posn. 3/50

General: *Has achieved very good fitting results through hard work and keen interest in all forms of class work. Can exemplary member in all ways.*

T. Pearson   *A.W. Branson*

Head.   Class Teacher.

My leaving report even says I have a happy cheerful manner!

LATCHMERE

Report on: Jacqueline Aitken Form: 4

Term ending: July 26th. 1957.

English: Reading: 49/50

Spelling: 22/25

Written Work:
Formal 47/50
Composition 47/50

Arithmetic: Mental: 21/25

Written:
Mechanical 50/50
Problem 47/50

Very good

Excellent progress

Art & Handwork:
Good

P.T. & Games:
Good

Exam. total 283/300
Class posn. 3/48

General: Has made excellent headway and achieved results of the highest standard throughout. A happy, cheerful manner makes her a valuable member of any class!

Class Teacher.

I seemed to have done surprisingly well in my arithmetic exams. I have a horrible feeling I might well have been copying off Marion again. I see I was third in the class. I know Julian was top and I think Robert was second.

I was brighter than I'd realized. I didn't really excel academically at my secondary school, Coombe. I made friends with a girl called Chris on my first day there, and we're still great friends all these years later. I don't mention her in *Jacky Daydream* as we didn't meet until we were eleven. However, lots of Chris's friends who read the book have assumed she's the Christine I was so close to in Mr Branson's class. It's so much less confusing if you write fiction – you'd never write about two friends with the same name! Chris asked recently if I was going to write about our teenage years. She sounded interested but a little apprehensive!

I can't decide whether to write another volume of autobiography or not. There's certainly plenty to write about. Maybe I'm a bit worried about setting a bad example! I didn't

work hard enough at school, I left home at seventeen and was married at nineteen. I wouldn't advise any girl to do that now!

I was still a compulsive daydreamer throughout my teens, writing endless stories. My first school photo at my new school Coombe shows me with pen in hand, writing in my notebook. I think

I must be eleven in the photo because my school uniform still looks remarkably new and neat. My hair is still short and permed, but I tried hard to grow it over the next few years. I often gave up in despair when it got to that irritating straggly stage and had it all cut off. Then I wouldn't like the new short haircut either and I'd start growing it all over again.

My hair's a little longer in this photo of Chris and me when we were about fourteen. I think that photo was taken in Chris's house. I always loved to go there because her family life was so placid and peaceful. Hetty and Fred, her mum and dad, were very fond of each other, her big sister Jan was very kind and friendly, even the budgie Joey chirped at me in a cheery fashion. Biddy and Harry were rowing more than ever by then.

This is me a year later, on
the balcony at Cumberland
House. My hair's now in a
weird overgrown bouffant
style because my boyfriend,
Peter, was a hairdresser and
used to practice on me. I
had quite a few boyfriends
but Peter was my first serious one. Here we are in
Peter's flat – and my hair's
even fancier now!

It looked as if my life was all mapped out. At sixteen I was sent to technical college to learn Shorthand and Typing because Biddy thought I should get a job as a secretary. I didn't want to be a secretary. I didn't want to settle down in Kingston and marry Peter. I wanted to be a writer and lead a glamorous arty life in a picturesque book-filled garret. But it all seemed a little-girl daydream . . . until I found an advert in the London evening newspaper saying 'Wanted! Teenage Writers!' I was a teenager and I desperately wanted to be a writer, so I wrote off for further information. The Scottish firm DC Thomson, who publish many newspapers and magazines and children's comics like the *Beano* and the *Dandy*, had decided to produce a brand new full colour teenage magazine and were eager for material for it.

I was certainly eager to write so I sent them off a humorous article. To my astonishment they wrote back saying they wanted to publish my piece, and would pay me three guineas for it. Even in those long ago days in the nineteen sixties three guineas (£3.15p) wasn't a lot of money, but it meant the world to me. Someone actually liked my writing and wanted to buy my article and publish it!

I wrote them a story or an article almost every day. After a month or so, DC Thomson offered me a job as a junior journalist in their Dundee offices. I jumped at the chance!

Biddy was a bit worried about me going up to Scotland at the age of seventeen and insisted I live in a hostel so that someone could keep an eye on me. I booked myself into the Church of Scotland Girls' Hostel. The matron didn't want to take me at first as all her rooms were full, but she saw I was quite small and squeezed a put-u-up bed into the linen cupboard and turned it into a weeny bedroom for me. This was a brilliant move because it was freezing cold that winter and the hostel didn't have any central heating. My linen cupboard had hot pipes to air the clothes and was the only cosy room in the huge mansion. All the girls wanted to be my friend so they could squeeze into my room with me. We used to squash up together, giggling in the dark, having midnight feasts just like those girls in the Enid Blyton boarding school books.

This is a photo of all us girls at the hostel's Christmas party (no boys allowed, and no alcohol either!). I'm in the back row on the far right.

Here's another photo of me in the office at DC Thomson – I think I was modelling knitwear for one of the women's magazines. I was willing to turn my hand to anything. I even wrote a weekly horoscope, though I knew nothing about

astrology. I basically made it all up! I'm born on December 17th which makes me Sagittarius, so when I was writing the column, all Sagittarians were going to have an exciting love life, come into lots of money and achieve all their ambitions.

Well, it's more or less all come true for me, though it took a long long time!

Here's a photo of me on my wedding day, marrying Millar. I look like a child, much too young to know what I was doing!

This is me a couple of years later, with my lovely daughter. I must have been about twenty-two then. I'd already written three or four unpublished novels, but I was still feeling my way. I was just about to write my very first children's book . . .